THE HUNGRY FORTIES

Cobden and Free Trade Literature.

THE STANDARD BIOGRAPHY.

THE LIFE OF RICHARD COBDEN.

By the Right Hon. JOHN MORLEY, M.P. With Photogravure Portrait from the Original Drawing by LOWES DICKINSON.

JUBILEE EDITION. 2 vols. 7/- the set.

POPULAR EDITION. 1 vol. 2/6 net.

ABRIDGED EDITION. Paper Covers. 6d.

THE POLITICAL WRITINGS OF RICHARD COBDEN.

A New Edition. With Preface by Lord WELBY and Introductions by Sir LOUIS MALLET and WILLIAM CULLEN BRYANT, and a Bibliography. With Frontispiece. 2 vols. Uniform with the Jubilee Edition of Morley's "Life of Cobden." Crown 8vo, **7/-** the set.

BRITISH INDUSTRIES UNDER FREE TRADE.

Essays by leading Business Men. Edited by HAROLD COX, late Secretary of the Cobden Club. Large crown 8vo, **6/-.**

LABOUR AND PROTECTION.

Essays by JOHN BURNS, G. J. HOLYOAKE, SEEBOHM ROWNTREE, and others. Edited by H. W. MASSINGHAM. Large crown 8vo, **6/-.**

THE OPPORTUNITY OF LIBERALISM.

By BROUGHAM VILLIERS. Paper covers, **1/-** net.

FISCAL REFORM SIXTY YEARS AGO.

Extracts from the Speeches of the Right Hon. Charles Pelham Villiers. Selected by WILBRAHAM VILLIERS COOPER. Paper cover, **1/-.**

CORN LAW RHYMES, and other Verses.

By EBENEZER ELLIOTT. Cloth, **6d.** Paper covers, **2d.**

MR. BALFOUR'S PAMPHLET: **A REPLY.**

By HAROLD COX, late Secretary of the Cobden Club. Price **2d.** net.

THE POLICY OF FREE IMPORTS.

A Paper read at Liverpool on 16th February, 1903, to the New Century Society. By HAROLD COX. Paper covers, **6d.** net and **1d.**

COBDEN'S WORK AND OPINIONS.

By Lord WELBY and Sir LOUIS MALLET. Cloth, **3d.**

FREE FOOD AND FREE TRADE.

By DANIEL GRANT, ex-M.P. for Marylebone. Paper covers, **2d.**

T. FISHER UNWIN, PATERNOSTER SQUARE, LONDON.

DES.D & DRAWN ON STONE BY R.L.SLY 61 SHAFTESBURY STREET NEW NORTH ROAD, HOXTON

THE FAIRY WHEATSHEAF,

OR

FREE TRADE & PROTECTION CONTRASTED.

This Print contains FAITHFUL LIKENESSES of the following

FREE TRADERS,

LORD RADNOR __ Mʳ VILLIERS __ THE LATE EARL SPENCER
THE QUEEN __ LORD ASHLEY

Mʳ SHIEL __ Mʳ BRIGHT __ Mʳ COBDEN __ LORD MORPETH __ COL. THOMPSON
Revᵈ SYDNEY SMITH __ LORD JOHN RUSSELL __ SIR R PEEL __ SIR J GRAHAM __ Dʳ BOWRING
· EARL GREY __ D OF WELLINGTON __ Mʳ O CONNELL __ LORD BROUGHAM __ Mʳ WILSON

PROTECTIONISTS,

LORD STANLEY __ D OF RICHMOND
LORD G. BENTINCK __ D OF BUCKINGHAM __ D OF NEWCASTLE __ Mʳ HUDSON
Mʳ FERRAND __ Mʳ DISRAELI __ D OF BEAUFORT __ D OF NORFOLK

London Published by C Edmonds 154 Strand.
three doors east of Somerset House.

THE HUNGRY FORTIES

LIFE UNDER THE BREAD TAX

DESCRIPTIVE LETTERS AND
OTHER TESTIMONIES FROM
CONTEMPORARY WITNESSES

WITH AN INTRODUCTION
BY MRS. COBDEN UNWIN, *editor*

ILLUSTRATED

LONDON: T. FISHER UNWIN
PATERNOSTER SQUARE. 1904

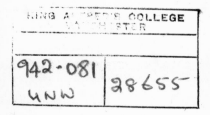

To

THOSE WHO IN

HIS NATIVE VILLAGE OF HEYSHOTT

HAVE KNOWN AND LOVED RICHARD COBDEN

THIS VOLUME IS

DEDICATED

CONTENTS

CHAPTER III.

CHAPTER IV.

CONTENTS

LIST OF ILLUSTRATIONS

THE BIG LOAF AND THE LITTLE LOAF.

(Facsimile of a Letter from Richard Cobden.)

Do not let the Borough
go uncontested. — I feel
quite sure that it will
be almost impossible for a
any bread taxer to be
returned in any town —
The women & children will
drive him from the field.
You should get some
handbills & tracts from
the League, at Manchester
for distribution in both
town & County. — The
best kind of placards

d handbills are the
pictorial ones, representing
the great & little loaves.

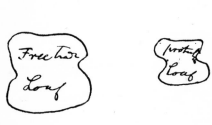

Free trade
Loaf

Protection
Loaf

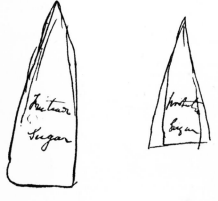

Free trade
Sugar

Protection
Sugar

INTRODUCTION

"IF I was to tell yer all the trouble in me life this room wouldn't hold it," said Widow Sanders in reply to the question, "Do you remember the old days of Protection, and the dear bread, Mrs. Sanders?" "Remember them! law bless yer, yes, my dear," was her reply. "Me and me husband and eight children to bring up on nine shillun' a week, and bread 1s. 2d. a loaf! Remember it!—why, many's the night I've gone to bed hungry, so the children might get me bit o' bread between 'em. Sorry the threshin'-machine makes that 'ummin' noise just this time o' year? Ye wish we 'ad the stroke o' the old flail back agin, do ye say? Ah! Many a time I listened for them strokes in the barn be'ind our cottage, afear'd they'd stop, and I know'd me husband 'ad dropped from the 'ard work and the empty belly. No, I'd raather 'ave the hum of that 'ere thresher, that I would." This little talk with my old friend, now at rest under the rose-trees in the peaceful Cocking churchyard, set me thinking, and gave me confidence—when the bread tax was imposed, now nearly two years ago—that rural England would have none of it. And recent events have, I think, proved that agricultural England prefers better clothing and better feeding to all the imaginary benefits to be derived from a policy of Retaliation, Preference, or Protection. And it was experience and knowledge of country life, coupled with Lord Rosebery's remarks, that suggested the issue of the following letter, which appeared in many newspapers in town and country :—

Sir,—Some time since I read in the press a letter from Lord Rosebery suggesting that those who remembered the miseries of Protection should lose no opportunity of telling their fellow-countrymen their experiences. He went on to say that in his judgment it was a clear duty they all owed their country, and their testimony would be of far more avail than the speeches, however eloquent and persuasive, of a younger generation, and that if they would stand on platforms and testify with regard to the facts of Protection, they would render an inestimable service at the present time.

I trust that many have carried out his suggestion on the public platform, but it occurs to me that there must be many who are in possession of private documents and diaries, illustrative of the bad old times, or who, from age and experience, might prefer rather to write down in simple language their recollections and experiences. Tradesmen's bills and private house-keeping accounts of the " Hungry Forties " would also be of interest and useful for comparative study. Some interesting documents of the kind have already appeared in the public press, and, as I am making a collection of such documents, I should esteem it a great favour if any of your readers would contribute any they may possess. I can promise that if I receive a good response to this suggestion I will publish the results in volume form in the interests of the cause of Free Trade, which all your readers, I feel confident, have much at heart. Let me add that any documents addressed to my care will be copied and returned if desired.—I am, sir, yours truly,

T. Fisher Unwin.

11, Paternoster-buildings, London, E.C.,
February, 1904.

In response a large number of replies have
been received in the shape of letters, diaries
and statements written by men and women
who, for the most part, have lived in rural
England prior to the abolition of the Corn
Laws.

To this material has been added a selection
of letters which have appeared in the public
press during the last year, the writers of which
may feel confident that they have contributed
a part to turn back the tide of Protection.

It has been felt that the contributions should
be printed as they were originally received;
they have not been edited except to remove
to a small extent portions not relevant to the
work in hand. These letters, veritable human
documents—"the short and simple annals of
the poor "—speak for themselves, and bear
indelible proof of their sincerity.

In Chapter III. communications from the
south of England are printed, and it will be
noted that comparatively few have come
from the county of Sussex and from this
part of England.

This may be partly attributed to the fact that the letter above quoted did not widely appear in the southern press—and to the fact that the feelings of the people in these districts have not been roused by stirring bye-elections.

The following conversations with village friends may somewhat help to fill the gap. They are simple, unvarnished stories as related by neighbours, and their personal characteristics will add interest and give Sussex colouring to this chapter.

Charles Robinson, Woodman, Heyshott Village.

" I was eighty-three years old only last week. My father came into this cottage to live when I was seven year old, and I was born in the village, and my parents before me. In my younger days the wage was not more than 9s. a week for work in the fields ; parish work was only 7s. Sometimes when we could get work in the woods, then we made as much as 14s. a week, but that was working by piece.

"You ask what sort of food we had. Well, crammings was common. It was made of what was left after the flour and the bran was taken away, and what was left, mixed with a little bread flour, we called crammings, but more often we made a sort of pudding with it. At that time, in the forties, in these parts we paid 1s. 2d. for a 'alf-gallon loaf, equal to two quarts ; 17s. a bushel, again, was the price for flour. This is about what we earned and what we 'ad to pay when I was married, away back in 1847. Some one said to me, 'If you can marry on that, then you will always be able to keep her.'

"You ask 'ow the people did get on. Well, they got into debt, and then again they lived on 'taters' and kept pigs, but butcher's meat we never 'eard of, never saw it except in the shops. Salt was 21s. a bushel, and when we killed a pig we 'ad to sell 'alf of it to buy the salt to salt down what was left. Then I remember my father would go out and up on to the common of a night to see if any fires was about. That was because the people burnt the ricks and barns in those days. But that was all a long time ago.

"Yes, I 'ave worked at Dunford, the only bit of work I did for Mr. Cobden, and I 'elped to make the new road by Hackett Gate, and I worked for ten weeks.

"You ask about cloes. Well, when I was a young man working people never did 'ave coats on; they are much better now. In those times they wore smocks, now you don't see them except amongst the Gypos people. They are the only people now that wear a smock, but I did see one at Oatscroft at a meeting there on the 3rd of June. Yes, people are better off now than in those days. I don't think we shall go back to them, and if they do they won't trouble me much at my age."

And then his daughter broke in and re-marked that even when she was a young girl, forty years ago, sugar was 8d. a pound. Tea, well the mother used to buy 2 oz. for 6d., which had to last a week for six people, and then to make it last out she would burn bread and mix the black crusts with the tea.

David Miles, Labourer, Heyshott
Village.

"Ay, I reklects the early forties afore the Corn Laws wor repealed. 'Taters was what folks lived on then, an' the Tories' ud 'ave it that a red 'errin' and a 'tater wor good enuff for any workin'-man. When I wor just on twelve the 'taters failed, an' never shall I forgit 'ow the folks went a-wanderin' about, peerin' at the 'taters, and tryin' to find out what wor wrong wi' 'em. It wor awful bad for the low class; many on 'em were nigh starvin'. If 'ee complained to the masters, they on'y said, quite indiff'rent, ''Ee can go; we don't want 'ee.' An' if 'ee went to the vestry, which they wor every blessed one on 'em farmers, and said as 'ow 'ee wanted work, they'd ask, 'Who've 'ee bin a-workin' for?' an' when 'ee answered, 'Mr. So-an'-so,' up the farmer 'd get and declare 'ee was dissatisfied, and then ne'er a one 'ud have anythin' more to do with 'ee. 'Twas ne'er a bit o' good leavin' the parish; they'd ask 'ee where did 'ee be come from, and when 'ee said, 'Heyshott,' they'd say as 'ow they didn't want no furriners, and that there ud be the end o't. It worn't no manner o' good a-tryin' to raise yerself, 'ee wor just a slave, and that's the truth. Them what cudn't get work 'ad to go on the parish or starve. Nowadays there's a many what 'a'n't got no manner o' notion what Protection is and think they'd like to 'ave a taste o't, but we old 'uns, we knows—lor' bless 'ee! we knows. Folks call 'em the good old times; that's just their ignorance; I call 'em the bad old times I do, when a few got fat and 'unnerds starved. If Mr. Cobden 'adn't got 'em Corn Laws repealed there'd 'ave bin a reg'lar Civil War in this yer country years ago. Folks used to put up a little 'ill o' taters for the winter, not two rods from their winders, but people 'ud come by night and steal 'em. A 'ungry belly makes a man desprit. They'd steal a'most anything, even bees and brocli from the garden. When a man 'ad a large fa'am'ly, they were pretty nigh starvin' mostly; as for meat, a look in at the butcher's shop was all theeir share o' that. The 'oomen ud cut off the black crust from the loafs and put it in the teapot and pour water on it instid o' tea; it looked pretty much the same colour, d'ye see; or else they'd beg the tea-leaves from the big houses.

"Ten hours a day is what we worked, a-threshin' corn in the barn. 'Twas hard, wearin' work; two o' us 'ud do it together; and 'ee 'ad to keep in turn, I can tell 'ee, or 'ee got a taste o' your neighbour's flail on the side o' yer face; many a one's got a black eye for threshin' out o' turn. Them that cudn't get work 'ud sometimes fire the barn. I got a job once six an' a 'alf mile away, and that seemed a fair step, I can tell 'ee, when I come 'ome tired of an evenin'; but I used to pass a 'ooman on the way what 'ad to dig up turmuts wid white frost on 'em, and I wouldn't 'a 'ad 'er job, bless 'ee, for a pound a week, that I wouldn't. 'Oomen used to 'ave to go a-weedin' in the corn in them days.

"When Mr. Cobden come 'ere Tiller and fifteen more wor a-breakin' stones on the road

for eightpence a day, that's just all they cud
get; but Mr. Cobden 'e altered all that. I and
some other youngsters 'ud meet 'im sometimes
when we wor a-goin' to school; 'e didn't take
much notice o' we; 'e allus seemed in a deep
study. I've thought since that 'e wor just
a-plannin' some good for 'is fellow-creatures.
I reklects when I an' my brother wor a-goin'
to school 'ow we'd see the big loaf for
Free Trade and the small loaf for Protection
stuck up in one o' the winders, and my brother
'e sez, 'Well,' he sez, 'the big loaf's the
best.''

CHARLES ASTRIDGE, EX-POSTMAN FOR
MIDHURST AND DISTRICT.

"For nearly fifty years I was postman in
Midhurst and the district. For twelve year I
walked eight mile a day, out to one of the
farms, and got three-and-sixpence a week.
There worn't many letters in those days.
Then another farmer, he offered me sixpence a
week if I'd go on a bit further and take his
letters; and then another, he offered me three

guineas a year to do the like, and I took all I could get, yer know, for 'twas hard livin' in those times. We had to pay 7d. for a half-quartern loaf; and many a time I remember lookin' in at the butcher's shop at the shoulders of mutton, but I never 'ad the money to buy 'em. The farmers in these parts used to pay their men 9s. a week. I remember meetin' a man named William Denyer one day what worked for Mr. Sadler, a farmer at Bepton, an' I said to him, ' I want to ask 'ee somethin' and 'ee needn't answer if 'ee don't want to '; and he said, ' What is it? ' and I said, ' I've heard as 'ee've been seen sittin' under the hedge with never a thing but bread an' apple for dinner '; an' he said, ' It's true, every word of it, s'elp me God! ' Often on a Saturday I'd see Jonathan Heath, what was the son of a wheelwright who lived in the Petersfield Road an' had a large family, comin' along with a penny bag of crammin's— that's what they give the pigs nowadays—to make the Sunday puddin' with. We mostly lived on bread, but 'twasn't bread like 'ee get now; 'twas that heavy and doughy 'ee could pull long strings of it out of your mouth. They called it growy bread. But 'twas fine compared with the porridge we made out of bruised beans; that made your inside feel as if 'twas on fire, an' sort of choked 'ee. In those days 'ee'd see children from Duck Lane come out in the streets of Midhurst an' pick up a bit of bread, and even potato peelings; y'ee'd see them do that. We can laugh at these things now, but it was no laughin' matter then. I can remember some twenty years ago carryin' letters for the Midhurst auctioneer round by Graffham and neighbourin' villages. And comin' round home by Heyshott church-yard that night I seemed somehow to hear the groans of them lying there in the churchyard who had suffered so much in their lives from privation. But things altered after Mr. Cobden come, and never shall I forget the day, about a week after the Corn Laws had been repealed, seein' Mr. Hall, the baker from Chichester, comin' along the village street with a cart full of half-quartern loaves, which he sold for fourpence each; he didn't take many back with him to Chichester, I warr'nt you. I can see him now in his black hat and white round frock—cow-gowns we used to call 'em.

"I often saw Mr. Cobden, sometimes a-walkin', sometimes in his old basket chaise, as 'e called it, and sometimes ridin' with one of 'is daughters. I never heard him speak but once, and that was at the Angel, for the Lancashire Relief Fund. Mr. Mitford 'e was there too, what was M.P. for Midhurst. Mr. Cobden 'e spoke first; 'e just raised his hand and rested it on the table and said, 'Gentlemen, I've no doubt many of you 'ere think I'm come 'ere to talk politics to you, but I'm not goin' to do anythin' of the kind. When I come down 'ere I feel just like one of Barclay and Perkins's dray-horses out to grass, and want to kick up my heels and sniff the fresh air.' It made us laugh, I can tell you. Mr. Cobden 'e did a lot for us, and 'e did a lot for others; 'e was just the greatest hero what there ever was in the world, and that's my firm belief."

Thomas Wrapson, Wood-sawyer, Heyshott Village.

" I call meself a wood-sawyer, but lor' bless my soul, I've bin in all sorts o' trades; anythin' that'll bring in a little money. It's a lot better now than it wor when I wor a boy; 'twor 'ard then for every one, an' that's the truth—nothin' but the truth. I've bin through the hoop meself; I'd more sense than some, but I've bin through the hoop. I don't want to see such times agen. We 'ud go out i' the fields an' sneak turmuts, an' 'ave 'em for supper wi' a bit o' bread. Of course I caant speak for out-landish places, but 'twor like that 'ere when I wor a boy. My father, 'e sez, 'If yer get snitched, yer'll get the birch rod.' I'd very little schoolin', an' when I fust went out to work I'd do a lot for a penny. I'd get a penny for carryin' water; many an' many a pail o' water I've carried up the hill for a penny, ay an' even a 'a'penny. Sometimes I wor in luck, an' got the use of a barrel an' a wheelbarrer, an' then I'd get tuppence. Time an' agen I'd

walk to Singleton an' back for a penny or
two, to fetch medicine-stuff from Dr. Turner,
the parish doctor, an' that's a matter o' more'n
eight mile. One time I got work up in the
old medder where the owls builds ; I worked
there for threppence a day, spreadin' the
manure and pickin' stones; and arterwards, I
did swede cuttin'.   Then there wor the leasin'.
We daren't go in the field afore they blew the
horn, then we got what we could. If 'twor
only a little, we rubbed it out an' threshed
it out ourselfs as well as may be, an' put it
in a pot with a pennorth o' milk and a slice
or two o' turmut an' boiled it up, an' then we
each ud take a spoon and help ourselfs. If
we got as much as a bushel o' leasins' we took
it to the mill to be ground, an' made it into
bread. When we got a 'errin' once an' agen
we thought ourselves mighty lucky. I minded
the sheep sometimes, an' got threppence and
fourpence a day for it.   Dear, oh dear ! wages
wor terrible low in them old days.

"One farmer never gave more'n a shillun a
week to 'is carter, and 'e'd got three or four

'orses to mind, a shillun a week an' their board, and some farmers they give eighteen-pence and their board, that's what many a one got, an' the farmers thought they wor well paid.

"The best thing in them days was the 'lotments. There wor a field o' old Lord Leconfield what wor let out in 'lotments o' half-acre and quarter-acre pieces, an' folks ud have so many rods for corn and so many for 'taters. They had to pay 3s. 9d. for a quarter of a' acre. Some folk ud keep pigs, an' the missus ud go round sellin' the lean meat to get money enough for the 'alf bushel o' salt to salt the pig down wi'. Lor' bless me, I remember it as if 'twas yesterday. Old Lady Egmont would give 'em a bit o' fish or puddin' or summit when they wor a-payin' the wages. She'd 'ave a pleeceman to keep off the childern, but that worn't much good, for she made 'em worse by throwin' 'a'pence for 'em to scramble arter. Yus, wages wor low then, but few 'ad the 'eart to leave Heyshott; they was afeard of them outlandish parts.

Young gells 'ud go out leasin' with ne'er a stockin' on their feet, splotch, splotch along with plenty o' water goin' into their shoes an' plenty o' water runnin' out, an' an old bit o' white string instid o' laces, an' their petticuts half-way up their knees. When they took the censhum they found there wor about three 'undred people in Heyshott in them days; I blieve there be about four 'undred now. What we mostly cared about wor to keep off the parish. But things changed, I can tell 'ee, when Mr. Cobden come. I wor a-workin' then at Bex mill, for tenpence a day, an' Mr. Frederick Cobden, who'd often be passin', 'ud say, 'Well, young Wrapson, why don't 'ee get somethin' better to do?' an' I didn't know what to answer; an' then Mr. Cobden 'e took me on an' paid me two shillun a day, 'e did. Wages was riz all round; them that used to work for 7s. a week, Mr. Cobden he give 12s. an' 15s. a week to, an' o' course the farmers 'ad to riz their wages too, or they'd 'a found themselves wi'out any men. Lord bless my soul, it made a sight o' difference, it did. I never stole no turmuts arter that, though I'd never been persecuted for't. Mr. Frederick Cobden 'e paid the wages. I often saw Mr. Cobden about, an' sometimes 'e'd speak to me, but more often than not 'e'd be sunk that deep in studdy that 'e never noticed nobody ; 'e seemed allus a-plannin' something.

"Do I recollect that young chap what they called Dani'l the Prophet? Why, o' course I do. We married 'is father by 'scription. When a young 'ooman got into trouble in them days, instid o' sendin' 'er to the poor-'ouse, they married 'er by 'scription. Some on us give tuppence and some on us thruppence, just what we could aford, an' paid the fees, an' got some bread an' cheese and beer for the weddin' feast ; an' when 'twas over the new missus she took an' tied up what wor left o' the bread an' cheese an' took it 'ome for to have on the morrer, an' when that wor gone I 'spect they 'ad to dig for turmuts. They lived in a little hut at the back o' the village, but they couldn't pay no rent, an' it 'ad to come out o' the rates. But Mr. Cobden 'e took 'e on, an' then they wor all right; many a cold mornin' they'd 'a' 'ad if it 'a'n't a been for 'e.

"The sayin' goes that 'ee should help the lame and the lazy, but that's not what I think, nor more it ain't what Mr. Cobden did; there's them that'll stand at their doors all day from nine o'clock till noon, an' put their finger in their eye an' play poverty, an' I'm not sayin' as how I wouldn't help 'em, if so be they 'ad no supper, but what I sez is, help 'em what does their best, an' them 'twas what Mr. Cobden 'elped, though I'm not denyin' that 'e had a soft place in 'is 'eart for them that be lame an' maybe lazy."

GEORGE POLLARD, LABOURER, HEYSHOTT
VILLAGE.

"Yus, m'm, I'm pretty well, thank you; I can get about, an' the more people get about the better they be, seems to me. I b'lieve I wor born at Graffham, but I can't 'zactly reklect what year 'twas. Mr. Manning [Cardinal Manning] wor the minister there when I wor a boy; 'e wor a nice sort of man. All the schoolin' that ever I got was at Graffham school. Connor wor the name o' the teacher; 'e'd been a bit o' a woodman or steward to the Bishop [Wilberforce], but 'e give it up an' took to the teachin'. I come back to Heyshott in my young days. I've done all sorts o' work in my time, movin' about from place to place, just where I could get most. I used to go cow-mindin' an' bird-mindin' at thruppence a day, or one an' sixpence a week. Sometimes I even went as far as Lunnon, grass-mowin', to Wandsworth and Wimbledon. That was afore the machines come in. Another time I used to go a-diggin' stones on Heyshott Hill; that wor when I wor married an' 'ad three chillun'; I wor workin' for the parish then, an' all they 'lowed me to earn wor 5s. a week. I could have done more easy, but they wouldn't pay for 't. Those wor hard days. My wife she 'ud go out in the fields a-weedin' an' a-stone-pickin' at tenpence a day ; or she'd go leasin' in harvest time and pick up p'r'aps a bushel o' corn, an' take it to the mill an' they 'ud change it for a little flour ; then she 'ud mix it wi' crammin's an' make it into bread.   Most o' the cottages 'ad their own ooven ; but we wor nigh starved sometimes, an' if 'twan't for the hares runnin' about the hills, an' a rabbit now an' agen, I dunno where we'd 'a bin.   No, we didn't see much tay in them days ; we couldn't aford it ; 'twas thruppence an ounce ; what we did was to toast a bit o' bread at the fire until it wor as black as that coal, an' put it in the taypot an' pour water on't, an' that wor' all the tay we got.   'Taters was what most folks lived on in them days ; and what did we do when there wor no 'taters ? Well, m'm, we 'ad to do wi'out 'em.   'Twor rare an' difficult to get cloes thenadays, an' many an' many a time we 'ad to go ragged. Boots was worst ; yer can get two or three pair now for what yer could get one then ; pilted 'an 'eeled they cost from eighteen shillun to a pound.   There 'ad to be a little conjurin', I can tell 'ee, before we could get a pair. We had to save our pence for weeks an' weeks. Harvest wor the best time. I could make as much as fifteen shillun or sixteen shillun a week then; but sometimes I 'ad to walk a terr'ble way to get there. Time an' agen when I wor a-bringin' up me faamly, I had to take the chillun on my back an' carry 'em all the way to Singleton an' Pegham, an' down below Chichester, an' we all 'ad to sleep o' nights in the barn. That wor afore the railroads wor made. Another time I'd go timber-cuttin' at Arundel, an' once I went right down to the coast an' worked at the sea-wall, what kep' the sea out; an' that wor rare an' well paid for, that wor. Forty year an' more I lived up in Hoyle Lane. I reklects the time when they worked iron in this county, and the old foundry up by Foundry Pond. They'd melt the old iron there, but I never 'eard tell what 'twor made into.

"Things began to look up when Mr. Cobden come to this 'ere place; wages riz right up;

'e giv' more money an' so the farmers 'ad to give more too, or all the men ud have gone to 'e ; 'e giv' 'em plenty o' work. A rare sight of grubbin' 'e had done at the lower end of the farm w'ere all the trees wor. Many a tree I grubbed up there, an' planted t'other side o' the garden. I digged the drain along the road there, an' Mr. Cobden u'd come past an' arst me how I wor a-gettin' on, an' 'is little boy Richard along o' 'im times an' agen. A rare game 'un the little chap wor ; up to anythin'. I never saw the like. He 'ud go choppin' at the trees, choppin' some o' 'em right off, but nobody said nothin' to 'e, 'e only larfed an' said 'twor good for trade. I wor a-workin' up in the holler when Mr. Cobden died. I never caught a sight o' the funeral. Gadd know'd I'd be out o' work, so he told me to come up to 'is place, an' I caught ne'er a sight o' nothin'. Folks was rare sorry when Mr. Cobden died ; 'e did a power for Heyshott, 'e did ; 'e wor the best man what ever come here. We 'a'n't never had such bad times since.

"Yus, I wear a cow-frock still, but I dunno as any o' the neighbours wear 'em; p'raps they've forgotten how to make 'm. My missus she made mine; some cost about six shillun. I've wore it year in an' year out I dunno how long. My old missus she died four year ago come last March. She wor a good partner, she wor. I don't suppose I shall ever want another frock; this'll last my time, I reckon."

WILLIAM TILLER, WOODMAN, HEYSHOTT VILLAGE.

"Well, well, Heyshott's another place from what it wor afore Mr. Cobden come 'ere, an' Dunford too; why, all the ground round was nothin' but a quagmire; a man 'ad to walk a long way round them days, if so be 'e wanted to get into Heyshott. But when Mr. Cobden bought the place 'e didn't rest wi' it like that, not 'ee. 'E just went an' arsked 'ow many men there wor on the parish. I dunno now whether 'twas twelve or thirteen, but which-

ever 'twas they all had to go down to 'e the
very next marnin' an' 'e set 'em all to work
right orf to make a road; twelve shillun a
week 'e paid 'em, an' rose 'em too on that;
'em what 'adn't bin gettin' more'n eightpence
a day a-breakin' stones on the road. Nine or
ten of 'em 'e had a-workin' all the winter.
Long afore 'twor finished Mr. Cobden 'e 'ad
to be off somewheres, lecturin' I do beleeve,
an' the night afore 'e went, Quinnell, 'is man,
what 'ad bin gettin' a bit onaisy like, 'e sez to
'e, 'e sez, 'What about them men what's
a-workin' on the road?' 'e sez. 'Well,' sez
Mr. Cobden, 'they've got to work on the road,
an' get their wages reg'lar every Saturday
night,' 'e sez. 'But,' sez Quinnell, ''sposin' it
rains an' the work's stopped.' 'Well,' sez Mr.
Cobden, 'they get their wages just the same,'
'e sez, 'unless so be it starts a-rainin' for three
weeks right off,' 'e sez, a-larfin'. I never in all
my born days seed a better master than what
Mr. Cobden wor; never a hasty word—I never
seed 'e out o' temper. If anything wor wrong
'e'd just say, 'Don't let it occur again,' an

never nothin' more. If there wor any trouble among the men 'e'd put it right. Charles Poat, what 'ad a big faam'ly, looked as if 'e never got enuff to eat, so Mr. Cobden just made 'e go round to Dunford every day to get some dinner, that's what 'e did. 'E never took nothin' in hand but what 'e made somethin' out o't. But the farmers didn't like 'e at first. Ay, for sure, Mr. Cobden reg'lar made this place. Wages went up an' food went down after 'e'd been 'ere awhile, an' 'e would a-fared just like 'is workmen 'e would, for sure ; there never wor no pride about 'e, bless 'ee. Why, I 'members one day when 'e'd bin away a long time, in Ameriky I b'leeve' twas, 'e come down one day sudden-like ; I seed 'e a-comin' along the road where we wor a-workin', me' an' Quinnell ; an' when 'e got up to us 'e sez, ' What 'ave 'ee got for dinner?' an' Quinnell 'e sez, ' Not much, sir, just a bit o' bacon,' an' Mr. Cobden 'e sez, ' That's good enuff for me,' an' down 'e cum to the farm cottage an' 'ad 'is dinner along o' us ; there worn't no pride about 'e, bless 'ee."

Charles Tiller, Foreman Carpenter, formerly of Heyshott.

"Oh, I remember Mr. Cobden well. When he first come down to Heyshott things were pretty bad, I can tell you. A half-gallon loaf cost one-an'-tuppence, and a gallon one two-an'-four; and wages was low, terribly low. My brother, who had a wife an' ten children, on'y got nine shillins a week. 'Twas difficult for folks to live thenadays, I can tell you. They couldn't get proper bread for the children; 'twas made mostly of crammings for the fowls, and not a bit of fresh meat from one year's end to the other. Many an' many a one only had potatoes, though some fam'lies could keep a pig an' feed him on acorns and such-like, an' when he got about thirty stone, they'd kill him an' salt him down, an' he'd last all the winter and pretty well all summer too.

"Well, as I was a-saying, Mr. Cobden he come down, an' he went an' he looked over Dunford. It belonged to young Whitter then, and was as messy an old place as ever you see in your life.

Young Whitter he laughed when he heard Mr. Cobden was wanting it; he said, 'He ha'n't got half enough money to buy it, but he can look over it,' he said. You see, nobody knew who Mr. Cobden was; they'd never heard of him; they never read what's in the papers; why, you cudn't get a paper for less than threppence or fourpence. When he bought the place, folks began to talk and wonder who he was and what he was going to do; the farmers were terribly set against him when he first come. First thing he did was to dig a cellar, an' then he started right away and pulled down the house until there was on'y just a bit of it left, an' then he set to work an' built on a study and a dining-room and a parlour. He took me on as carpenter; I put in two big cupboards and did odd jobs. When Mr. Cobden first took me on, he called me into his room and he said, 'Tiller,' he said, 'there's one thing I want of you, and that is to be truthful and trustworthy,' he said. An' I said, 'Sir,' I said, solemn-like, 'you can depend on me,' and he smiled and said, 'That's all I want.'

He paid me fifteen shillings a week, he did, as carpenter. That was tip-top wages, and the other men what he took on he paid 12s. and 14s. and 15s., according to what they could do. Oh, 'twas very diff'rent, I can tell you, when Mr. Cobden come down. He was the best man that ever stepped in Heyshott, he was, an' nobody'll deny it. 'Twas he that made us all go to Night School. I was 'most twenty-seven then, and all the schooling that ever I had was at a dame school, Mrs. Baker was her name; she lived up the common. She couldn't write her own name, but she could read a bit an' she taught us to read. The one that read the fastest he was the best scholar; it didn't matter, lor' bless 'ee! whether 'twas right or wrong. When I was risin' nine, my father said I'd had scholarship enough, an' set me to work at the sawing, an' I haven't bin out of work more than a day ever since. But Mr. Cobden he made us all go to Night School, in Midhurst. He was a wonderful one for wantin' folks to get on in the world. He'd get places for us time an' again. He got my brother a place at Mr. Thomas Bazley's, an' he worked there till they made him head gardener. Once he got a good place for a brother an' sister together, but lor' bless you! when the time come they were afraid to leave Heyshott; they felt a sort of suspicious of other places. Times out of number he'd come an' have a word with me when I was a-workin' for him. He wanted me to go up to the great Exhibition (1851), but I'd never bin to London an' I said, 'I'd rather not.' But a lot of 'em went, an' when they came back, they gave me what for, I can tell you. Mr. Cobden he used to say to us, 'You young men ought to read the papers,' he said; an' we'd say, 'We haven't got money to buy 'em,' an he'd answer up quick, 'You could buy a paper instead of going to the public,' he'd say, 'an' then you'd see what is going on in the world, an' how you're put upon,' he'd say. An' if we answered that we couldn't read, 'Then get some one to read to you what can,' he'd say. Oh, he was a rare man for wanting folks to get on, Mr. Cobden was. When he was building his house I said to him one day, I said, 'What may you be wanting a study for, sir?' 'To study in,' he said; an' then he turned on me and said, 'Ha'n't you begun to study yet?' said he, 'for,' said he, 'if so be you hav'n't it's time you did,' he said.

"It appeared to me as how Mr. Cobden was so busy thinking about the country that he had never no thought for his own concerns."

MR. AND MRS. JENNER, HEYSHOTT VILLAGE.

"The first ever we 'eard of Mr. Cobden was one day when I was a-sittin' near the front gate and three men come along over the hill; they stopped when they saw me and arst me what was the name of the village, and when I said 'Heyshott' they brightened up and said as 'ow they'd been a 'untin' for it for a long while; they said they wanted Dunford, and I pointed 'em out the way and off they went; and as I passed by Dunford, Mary Tiller came a-runnin' out to me, and sez she, 'I wor just a-goin' up to Walker's to see Gran'ma and I see three strange men at Dunford, taking a top brick off the chimley of each of the cottages to take back to Mr. Cobden '—there wor three labourers' cottages there in those days; and I sez, 'Mary, that's a sign some one's bought the place an' is comin' to live 'ere; you mark my words,' I sez. An' sure enough before many days were over we 'ad Mr. Cobden down.

" Me 'usband 'ad a little cart in them days, drawn by two dogs, and 'e used to go into Chichester and buy fish and come back an' sell 'em in Heyshott. I can 'ear 'im now a-callin out, ' Fish, all alive-o!' He was a-walkin' it along one day when by came Mr. Frederick Cobden, and when 'e sees 'im 'e stopped an' 'e says, ' Well, I never know'd 'ee could get such fine fish 'ere,' an' 'e bought pretty nye the whole barrowful. An' by comes Mr. Cobden an' 'e stopped too, to see what wor goin' on; an' 'e sez to my husband, ' Yee're a strong, likely-lookin' man, can't yee get anything better to do than that? Come up to Dunford and I'll give yee something worth doin'.' Me 'usband 'e were fairly taken aback an' just mumbled out,

' When'll I come?' an' Mr. Cobden answers up sharp, ' To-morrow mornin'.' Well, my husband 'e come 'ome though 'twas still early in the mornin', an' 'e threw down on the table the money what Mr. Cobden 'ad given 'im, and that startled me, yee may be sure, for sure 'tworn't like 'im to give me the money till night; an' 'e give me the two fish what 'e had left an' 'e just says, ' Cook 'em for dinner, I'm goin' out,' an' out 'e went with never another word, leavin' me a-wonderin' what in the world 'ad 'appened. Just afore dinner 'e come back agen, and I 'eard my little girl a-cryin' out in the garden, ' Daddy's only got one dog, Daddy's only got one dog,' an' I run out, an' sure enough there was only one dog there, an' I sez to 'im, 'Whatever 'ave yee been a-doin'?' and 'e sez, ' I've sold me fish an' I've killed one of me dogs, an' now I am a-goin' to work like a man, praise God.' That was over fifty years ago. Me 'usband an' I 'adn't been married long then. I remember our weddin' day; we'd only been six weeks a-courtin', an' on our weddin' day me an' me husband, we reaped a whole acre of corn ; six shillun an acre was the price we was paid."

"We found it pretty difficult to live in those days afore Mr. Cobden come. Bread was one-an-threppence a quartern loaf, an' an ounce o' tea was sixpence ha'penny, an' sugar eightpence a pound, an' then 'twas so damp yee 'ad to dig it out with a spoon. Mr. Cobden 'e bought what they called the Town land and set to work makin' a road, an' 'e put me on to it ; my first job was grubbin' up the roots of the timber in Walkers' Field ; eleven shillen a week 'e give me, an' time an' again 'e'd send me wife down half a crown or a rabbit or summat. Afore Mr. Cobden come boys would work for tuppence or threppence a day, or one-an'-six-pence a week, mendin' the roads. The bread what we got couldn't hardly be called bread at all ; 'twasn't made o' flour, but just o' what remained after the best part o' the flour 'ad been taken away, an' often it was that stodgy an' damp yee 'ad to dig it out o' the middle with a spoon. Sheep's 'eads is what we mostly lived on ; we could get one for sixpence and two 'ud last us a week, made into soup ; but 'tworn't great shakes, I can tell 'ee. But Mr. Cobden 'e altered all that ; 'e was a good friend to us in Heyshott, that 'e was."

JOHN GOFF, CARTER (AGED 70), HEYSHOTT VILLAGE.

" Oh'a, I reclect the old days well enuff, I do—'leven on us to starve on nine shillin' a week. Seven to five o' nights I work'd when I wor a lad, an' liv'd mostly on cram-min's. Many a day we 'ad o' work on a swede turmut a-boil'd down, I declare ! Yer'd give one shillin' an' sixpence a loaf o' bread we 'u'd in them days. An' no tay—bread yer'd bake and po'r 'ot water on't an' drink. We cudn't get nothin' more.

" First I went a-work at a penny a day, an' they rose up to tuppence, an' up to six-pence at last when I wor ten year. When I got up to twelve year they giv' me one

shillin' and fourpence a week then. An'
then I got carter-boy an' they giv' me two
shillin' a week. That wor for ever so long.
Then it came to four shillin'. That wor
w'en I got made a milk-boy. An' w'en
I got four shillin' a week me faather thought
that fine, an' 'e'd say as 'ow we could 'ave
a extra loaf. I worked thirty-three year wid
one farmer.

" In them days there wor no butter as there
be on the table there, nor cheese more nor
once a week, for we cudn't get it; with a
piece o' bread we thought ourselfs in luck.
I can get enuff to eat now, I can. Then
many a night it were 'ard work a-gettin'
home, I wor that hungry. Now people tell
me we ain't no better off. Don't tell me!"

Then Mrs. Goff broke in, and told the
same story how her mother, Widow Sanders,
brought her and seven more up having, for her
only stock-in-trade, a recipe for excellent
catchup.

" Ah, many's the day I've spent with
mother a-lookin' for mushrooms by Hook's

Ways and the Devil's Jumps, round Harting way, till the prespration a-po'red from her. She was a good mother to us all." And then, after a hospitable cup of tea, to the accompaniment of fresh bread-and-butter, I left them to their comfortable evening meal, and in the twilight turned my steps homeward, pondering on the past and present lives of those old friends and neighbours in the little Sussex village under the " Dear South Downs."

*   *   *   *   *

These statements tell the same story as do those from other counties in England, and will, I trust, prove to be of permanent historical and documentary value, giving as they do vivid pictures of the life of rural England in the first half of the nineteenth century. At the same time they will be practical and effective antidote to the raging, tearing campaign of those who would by legislation bring England back to the times of the Hungry Forties.

J. C. U.

HEYSHOTT, SUSSEX,
            October, 1904.

PROTECTION IN THE MIDLANDS

CHAPTER I

PROTECTION IN THE MIDLANDS

THE letters in this chapter, coming as they do from the central counties of England, deal with a district in which the conditions under Protection, as now, were naturally more varied than perhaps in any other. The district is neither so purely agricultural as eastern or western England, nor yet so completely manufacturing as the North. The proximity of large towns exercises a favourable influence on agricultural wages by offering the rural labourers an alternative to field work. Hence, London and Birmingham being within reach of many of the counties with which we here deal, the poverty of the rural labourers was hardly quite so deplorable as that of which we have evidence in Devonshire and Dorset ; nor, considering its size and population, has the district been quite so eloquent.   Perhaps the following letter, with its quaint and picturesque detail, gives as good an idea of actual life conditions in "protected" England as any.   The details it gives as to wages, &c., are particularly clear.   The letter is dated February 12, 1904, from 14, Bouverie Street, Northampton :—

"I, Joseph Boddington, was born on May 27, 1827.   Our family consisted of 7 brothers, 2 sisters, father and mother.   I was the youngest but one.   Father hedge-cutter and thatcher, and all hard work of any kind.   I had to go to work with him at the age of six years old, weather hot or cold.   My little hands would suffer very much with the frost and coald.   We tried to live on barley-bread, but we could not do without mixing it with wheat-flour.   I worked with my father until I was 12 years old.   We had one of those large chimney fire-places—father on one side, mother on the other, room for 2 boys on

each side ; I would get on mother side. We
was not allowed free speech, so I would
just pull mother's face when at meals, and
then she would say, ' Boy, I cannot eat this
crust '; and O ! the joy it would bring into my
little heart. At night we would have a 3-leg
iron pot and a good dose of small potatoes, and
a little bit of fat to keep them from burning ;
and O ! the eyes and ears that watched and
listened to them as they were being roasted !
No fairy could have come down that big
chimney to have taken one of them potatoes—
we should have had her in a moment. At 12
I went to a farm lodge out of the village, to
work from 6 o'clock in the morning to 6 in the
evening. My wages up to 16 years old were
5d. per day—2/6 per week. Then I went to
another village, and set myself for 12 months
for the sum of £2 10 0. I was taken on the
next year £4 0 0. In my 19 year I set myself
for £4 15 0. When I was in my 24 year a
farmer came and offered me 6/6 per week.
The same year I helped a farmer get his hay
and harvest in, and then he said he could not

keep a single man on, so I went the next day and put the banns up in church, and then he sent for me and gave me the sum of 8 per week to get married on. I worked for him nearly 2 years. He gave me the sack because I asked the servant girl to go to chapel. I have seen 14 young, strong men stand in the village with nothing to do. One man said he had been three days at work, and they gave him 2/6 for the three days, the same time I worked 2 days for 2/6, and I told him I would have throwed it at him only I wanted it. The next day after he sacked me I got 2/- per day and never went back. I have now been a local preacher 50 years, but my work is nearly done ; but I can bless the good Lord at all times for His great love to me and mine. I have taken the *Christian World* almost from its commencement—it is from that I write to you. I might say, in conclusion, I have my third wife and she has her third husband. We have never claimed the Dunmow flitch of bacon, but I think we might have done. I do hope your book will be a very great success when sent out. I may subscribe myself as your unknown friend,

"JOSEPH BODDINGTON."

Our next letter is from Mr. Wm. Prestidge, of 28, Manor Road, Bishopston, Bristol :—

"I was born in the parish of Meriden, near Coventry, Warwickshire, 76 years ago, and can well remember those 'good old times,' falsely so called, as they were anything but good times to my dear father and mother and us 5 children. His wages were but 9/- per week, with 2 pence per day that I got for frightening the crows off a farmer's wheat, making another 11d. per week to keep seven of us, and father had to pay 6 pounds per year out of that for his house to live in, so you may guess how we lived with the 4-lb. loaf at 11½d. tea from 5 to 8 shillings per lb., and vile sugar at 9 pence per lb. Then meat—mutton, beef, and poultry—I don't know how they were sold—we could only see those things. One ounce of tea and a pound of bacon a week, with a dish or two of swedes thrown in, if we

could get them, as the potatoes were a great
failure after the disease set in, which has continued more or less ever since, and was the
cause of thousands of deaths in Ireland. And
from frightening the crows off the farmer's
wheat, when I got a bit older I used to help
father thrash out the corn, with two heavy
sticks swinging over my head all day, on
barley and wheat bread and small beer, in the
farmer's barn ; and we used to have 'tea-kettle
broth' for breakfast. What would the young
people think of such a breakfast as that to-day?
I never had a day's schooling in my life, but
was always brought up to behave myself lowly
and reverently to all my betters. My dear
father died at 43 years of age through hard
work, bad living, and other terrible hardships ;
and now Joseph Chamberlain wants to bring
us back to those good old times again with his
Fiscal Policy and Protection."

Though usually included among the Eastern
Counties, Hertfordshire, lying as it does between them and the Midlands, is perhaps,
for our purpose, more fitly included in our

present chapter. Substantially the conditions of life in Hertfordshire are more likely to resemble those of the neighbouring inland rural district, which includes the Midland Counties of Bedfordshire and Bucks, than those of the low-lying maritime counties further east. For this reason we have classed Herts as a Midland County, our object being in the main to keep together those districts where the industrial and agricultural conditions were most alike.

Interesting because of the venerable age of the writer was the following letter, sent by Mr. Richard Rigg, of Redbourne, to the agent for the Liberal Candidate during the Mid-Herts contest of 1904 :—

" I am an old man, in my hundredth year, and Protection or Free Trade will not injure or benefit me now, but I should like to tell you, in a few feeble words, of my experience under both laws.

" I was born in Maresworth, Hertfordshire, in 1804, and worked early. I remember bread then being 1s. 6d. a loaf. I worked as a plough-boy, with my mother's boots tied on to my feet with string. My first engagement was with a farmer, who, in return for my labour, gave me free food and no wages. When I was too ragged to be decent, my master applied to the parish for clothes for me. We used to wear sheepskin breeches, and when we got them wet through, we lay on them at night to dry them for morning. At sixteen years of age I worked for £5 a year, and received board free. At eighteen years of age I was getting £8 a year. In 1826 I married, and received 9s. a week wages, and as time went on my wife had four children, and we were half-starved, and my master reduced our wages to 8s. a week. However, I managed to get work on the first railway line being made, at Tring cutting, and left the farm work. I remember Lord John Russell's Reform Bill, and since then things improved. I can well remember Cobden and Bright agitating the country for Free Trade.

"Working men, don't forget your half a crown will buy nearly twice as much to-day as it did then. If you had lived in those dark, cold days, you would appreciate your blessings of to-day brought about by Free Trade. I respect the Tories, but disapprove of their ways and actions, and consider myself a great sufferer through them. I wish the Liberals every success. I have been a Liberal all my life, and see no reason to alter my opinion now I am old."

The writer of our next letter, which appeared in the *Daily Chronicle* for the 24th of February, 1904, gives what we believe to be the true reason for the fact that while almost every other kind of food was dearer, meat was cheaper during Protection days than at present. The fact is that there was then practically only a middle and upper class demand for beef and mutton. Some pork was bought for Sundays by the poor, but otherwise meat was altogether beyond their means, with the inevitable result of a restricted market and low prices.

" My personal recollections," says T. G. W., writing from Malvern, "go back to the time of the anti-Corn Law agitation.   When I saw, at a meeting here this winter, the big loaf and the little loaf displayed, I recognised old friends, for I had seen them carried in procession in the early forties.

" The condition of things then existing cannot be realised by the present generation. Bread has long been so cheap that the years of famine are forgotten or unknown. Bread has almost taken its place alongside of air and water, as things we have no special reason to be thankful for.   When I was a boy tenpence was a minimum price for the 4-lb. loaf, and often it was a shilling, and even then generally of very poor quality.   Other articles of ordinary consumption were correspondingly dear, sugar 10d. per pound, and very common tea 4s.   Only meat was cheap, because the working classes could not afford to buy it. When exceptionally bad harvests came, matters were worse.   In the potato famine year, 1845, I remember our trying to make potato flour by grating the half-rotten potatoes into a large tub full of water.   The white flour sank to the bottom and looked very nice, but I do not remember eating any of it. It was merely an interesting experiment for us, but the suffering amongst the working people was a very grim reality. Oatmeal in various forms and barley bread formed the staple food of the masses, and almost the only luxury they were able to indulge in was a red herring, the smell of which pervaded the air as you passed the workmen's cottages.

"I have often heard my father tell the following story : In the year 1802 there was a very poor harvest. In the manufacturing town in the South of Scotland where he lived the town crier went round one day to announce that there was wheat-flour for sale at a small flour mill a few miles off. Not to lose time, my grandfather, who was in comfortable circumstances, and the chief magistrate of his native town, at once sent off a man on horseback to secure a sack of this precious stuff. I cannot remember the price paid—it was something enormous—but when the so-called flour arrived it was so full of grit and dirt that it could not be used.

"In 1849 I entered the office in Liverpool of a merchant engaged in the China trade. One of my first tasks was to pay duty at the Custom House upon a chest of tea. The cost of the tea landed in Liverpool was under 10d. per pound—say £3 odd per chest—and the duty was 2s. 1½d. per pound, or £8 odd per chest. Did the 'heathen Chinee' pay that duty? Some people will say that he did! Well, this world would be a very uninteresting place if there were no fools in it.

"I was resident in America between the years 1884 and 1901, and on my return was quick to notice any apparent changes in our old country. Now, what has struck my wife and myself above everything else is the great improvement that has taken place in the apparent condition of the working classes. They are better dressed, have more and better food, and more leisure time than they used to have. It is surprising that this improvement has taken place during the years that have convinced Mr. Chamberlain that Free Trade was the device of two schemers or dreamers, named Cobden and Bright, and that Protection is the panacea for all our ills."

The following letter, which appeared in the *Daily News* of February 5, 1904, gives interesting details as to prices and wages, which bear out other evidence in this work :—

" SIR,—I wish to recall, for the benefit of the present generation, the bad times of Protection. My father's wages were 15s. per week, which was 4s. per week above that of the average working man. Bread was 10½d. per 4-lb. loaf; tea, 4s. 6d. per lb.; very common sugar, 6½d., which was adulterated with sand; and I may say all goods were very largely adulterated. Clothing was dear, and the working man had to dress in the coarsest of clothing. I can well remember having to turn into the fields at break of day gleaning, and my father, after a hard day's work, perhaps walking two miles to help to carry home our burden of corn, which was often sprouted at the end of harvest. This was sent to the mill and ground into flour. The bread which was made from the flour was nearly black, and I am quite sure the working man of to-day would not eat it. In those days the working man did not leave work at 12.30 on Saturdays. Bricklayers' wages were 3½d. per hour, and carpenters the same. I have no desire to go back to the days of Protection. Just imagine eggs, butter, meat, and all other things which we cannot do without, having a tax on them! Will the working men of this country listen to such a proposal? Why, sir, it will have just the opposite effect on trade; if these things are dear, people will have to do with less; consequently less trade.—Yours, &c.,

"W. H. Moss.

"Bournbrook, near Birmingham."

The next letter, from "A. J. M.," comes from Northampton. Unfortunately for our purpose the recollection of the writer, as he says, does not go back quite so far as those of most, for his account is remarkably complete as far as it extends. We print it practically entire, for the details of life given, even when not the result of the fiscal heresy of the time, are interesting :—

"My recollection takes me back into the fifties when, if bread was but slightly taxed, many other things were heavily burdened. Physically and intellectually we dwelt next door to destitution. The principal course at the morning meal would be a small basin of bread soaked in water, and seasoned with salt, occasionally a little skimmed milk added, and a small piece of bread tinged with lard in winter. During the summer season we might at rare intervals get some dripping from the Hall. For dinner we might get plain pudding—flour and water—or pork dumpling, sometimes both, with potatoes or onions added to fill the crust. The last course, except the dessert of potato soup, &c., might be potatoes and meat—pork— you should have seen the joint! We might get 2 lbs. per week. 'Tea,' such we called it, bread and potted butter. I never remember grumbling about this being sparingly spread, it was at times so rancid. 'Supper?' Well, sometimes I used to transgress by staying out late, so had to slip off without, or I might get something very much like a small piece of bread and a little piece of pork rubbed over it. Sunday was a high day, of course. We might get a penny black pudding[1] for breakfast, suet pudding and a pig's foot for five of us to feast thereon. Beef? Yes, we might get a small piece at our feast and a bullock's heart at Xmas. We did occasionally get a pennyworth of bullock's liver if we happened to be going to town—about 3 miles—for the doctor during the week. Beverage? Well, yes, we used to have as much as 4 oz. of tea and 2 of coffee for 3 weeks, 1 lb. of sugar per week. To illuminate our cottage in winter we would get half a pound of candles (10d.) and a rushlight for father to retire and rise with, as it did not consume so rapidly. As an additional drink we had mint-tea for summer, and we might get toast and water, especially when ailing, in winter.

"Then as to the news of the world. Our

---

[1] One between 4 or 5 of us, with a small piece of fried pork.

world extended to about 3 miles on either side. Father usually attended the town Chapel on Sunday mornings, and might get a scrap or two of information. Newspapers nil. Periodicals? About the same number. Books? Father and mother had a Bible and hymn-book and prayer-book. Such were some of the delights of those dear old days. Would that I could transport 'our Joe' and his jingo tribe where they could learn a common-sense lesson in the school of experience! We used as lads to play a game when one was called upon to pick out his fellows who had assumed another name, and when failing he would be instructed thus: 'Old fool, go to school and learn better wit.' I think this would be hard to beat for applying to fiscal fanatics. As to matters in general, the wages of labouring men would be about 10s. in summer and 9s. in winter. Many families would have to go into debt, trusting to extra pay in harvest and the gleanings of the family to enable them to pay the shoemaker, &c. Some would purchase tailing corn, and if a sheep or other animal died would perhaps get a part or the whole of the carcass on the cheap.

"Our dress for Sunday and week-day might be smock frock and corduroy. Small lads would set out to work some at 6, others might wait until 7 or 8, &c., and might get 1s. per week with the prospect of an annual rise of 3d. I did not commence until over 8, and had 3d. per day of 12 hours. I am still classed at 12 hours. I have heard a town tradesman talk as foolishly as a duke who bears my county's name about the folly of having cheap articles and no money to buy them. Within my recollection there was scarely a trade cart came into the village to call on labourers. Two vehicles we did see. The relieving officer used to come once a week —bread was then served out—and a peculiar shaped hearse to bring from the infirmary or workhouse the remains of a former resident. Go into the same village to-day and you may have to be on the look-out not to be run down by the vehicles of tradesmen and others. Yet the inhabitants are, I believe, considerably less. Others as foolishly talk about the time of

agricultural prosperity.   Such expose themselves more than they know.   Labourers not
only had to toil when they could get work, but
to tramp thereto.   I have known men to come
from a village said to be 8 miles distant for a
day's work at threshing.   Most villagers might
be employed during haytime and harvest before
machinery was much used, but at other times
many might walk miles for draining in winter
and for other things in summer.   Then as to
'the cottage homes of England.' A poet's fancy
would not harmonise with facts in many cases.
My earliest recollection is of 4 cottages in a
row, 5 over-head bedrooms, and representatives
of 8 families, two 2, one 3, and one 1.   Then
how were they furnished ? Many would have
a few rush-bottomed chairs, a few stools, and a
round deal table, some trenchers and wooden
spoons to match, with the sun to tell the time
of day, and 'Old Moore' for those who could
make out the time of the year.   Some were, of
course, a little farther advanced.   We had two
clocks, one with 1 hand, the other with two,
and I could tell a tale respecting one of these,

how its loss filled me with sorrow ; but that is beside the mark.

"Some are making much ado to-day about getting men back to the land. Know they what they say ?   In the village I reside in probably even more than $\frac{3}{4}$ of the toilers have to go out of the village to work, or are otherwise engaged than on the land.   There are, of course, many comfortable cottages and gardens throughout the land, still the inhabitants may be so hedged in with restrictions that might remind one of a S.A. compound.   A large number of others were probably built on waste by labourers, who might be glad to barter them for a shilling or two per week in old age, as they could get no parish pay while owning a house.   Many of these stand to-day, no credit to our country or to those who claim them. In some cases cottages stand back to back, or there may be front doors both ways, or one front door for two cottages ; then in many places village rents are being raised.   In many places, while there is ample room and protection for game, the poor are huddled together.

Many are workless in the country as well as the town ; only yesterday a young bricklayer was digging an allotment for me. England needs something more than a politician on pilgrimage with promises as profuse as his pledges are worthless. It needs a lover of God to step forth as a leader of men, to wean us from or smash our golden gods, and show that only by serving our generation can we do the will of God. There is need of a radical revolution ; the land should be the bedrock on which national burdens rest. Machinery used to lighten the labourers' lot rather than to supersede. Why should one have to toil half his living hours, and another have to wander workless, while a third reaps the reward ? In a word, we need a Co-operative Commonwealth, to fight *for* rather than against each other. If any part of the foregoing will be of service you are welcome thereto, only suppress name and whereabouts.—Yours respectfully,

"A. J. M."

The following excellent letter is from

Leicestershire : " I was born in 1836. I was sent into the fields to scare crows, and when I had done a full week, 7 days, I had one shilling. I was such a small boy my father carried me on his back to work. The corn was 105s. per quarter, bread 1/- per 4-pound loaf. My first week's money bought 1 loaf. I have had a little conversation with Mr. Thos. Binney, late of Padby, farmer. He told me his father refused 105/-, and rather than sell he kept it till the rats nearly devoured it, and then he had to sell it for 70/-. The farmer 'as never been the friend of the toiler. They are the most ignorant class of men in England. They have supported the very men who have crushed them. Why don't they go in for Land Law Reform? The are to thick-headed. This is just how they want to keep us, or why should they rob the people of public control? Men, wake up! You can't find an Englishman, only through his belly. I am close on 70 years of age. I shall soon be gone, but I will try to make the paths of men more smooth than what I found them. If every man done this, it would be a heaven instead of hell. In 1844 the Chartists were led by Ernest Jones; days I well remember. The farmer held the plough, the son drove, the daughter milked and assisted in the dairy. Do they do it now? Do you see a farmer with a ragged coat, a pale face, without a cigar, without horse or trap? No! Are we to rise the price of bread for a few 1,000 farmers and cause misery to 1,000,000? No! In 1844 men was brought to justice for sheep-stealing, sent to Van Demon's Land for 14 years. If you took a pheasant by night, 14 years. Two men in this village had 14, Jack Burrell and Bill Devenport. In 1844 it was not safe to go out after dark if you had any money on you. Burgaly, highway robbery, fowl stealing because men were starving. Men would steal sheep to get sent away. They had there freedom when they got there. When we have to be sent away as convicts to get liberty, we quietly sit down at home slaves. Shame on working men ! But where are the sheep-stealers to-day? The conditions of men is better—they have disappeared. But the men who made the men steal through Protection, hunger, and misery, and finding we had killed Protection and buried it, he has had to turn thief himself. Where ? On the Stock Exchange. In '45 Bright and Cobden was agitating England through for repeal of Corn Laws. Rioting was in every large town, and shops were guted. Rows of men chained together. I see as late as '53 men marched through Northampton streets to the gaol from Nottingham—there prison was full. It was said Nottingham Castle was in flames. Do you want to see this again ? These poor men had no votes. They were better without it than thousands to-day are with it. They made the Government repeal the Corn Laws. In the little borough I was born, Daventry, a gentleman the name of Jenkings every Monday would tell the town baker, named Kebble, to fill his oven as full as he could of small loaves. He would come at 6 in the

evening to distribute. I have se hundreds
of people stand 2 hours for fear should not
get one. Good old days! I was the oldest
of 7 children ; and when I was old enough
I crept into the wood by the light of the
moon, and brought out once 5 pheasants to help
to keep my father, mother, brothers, and sisters
from starving. In 1850 the corn went down.
The Crimean War it come up again to £5.
The farmer was the jackal for landlord. He
squeeze the labourer to 7/-, 8/-, 9/-, and 10/-
a week. The farmers wore a white smock
frock, the labourers a brown one—that was
there dress-up! Bricklayers had 18/- a week,
labourers 12/-, some 10/-, carpenters 18/-,
painters 18/-, blacksmiths 16/-. There was
no union ; it was according to supply and
demand. I was among the shoes. I have
seen the day in '46 when a man in the shoe
trade would give 2/6 for every man he could
get. To-day there are thousands would give
5/- to get them a job. And what is the cause
of this? A surplus labour market. When
I go home to Daventry I get and look at

the farm I first worked on. There was 15 men and wives and children, make no doubt 100 ; to-day there is one shepherd on that land.

"If a man is only getting 6/- a week he is better off than any father would be 60 years ago with 23/-. I will prove it. In '45, before the repeal, bread, 1/- 4 pound ; sugar, lump, 9d. ; currants, 6d. Before the Boer War corn, 16/- quarter, the lowest I ever knew, brown bread 3d. the 4-lb loaf, sugar 2d., currants 2d. Take the 6/- to-day, it would purchase what my father paid £1 3s. for. So much for Free Trade. If I live I am going to give an address on the days of Protection. I shall just be at home. I can speak, but I can't write.   " J. HAWKER.

"13, Cross Street, Padby."

We should naturally have expected to be able to give a whole chapter to London. The great city has, however, been remarkably silent, and we are driven to treat London, for the purposes of this book, as if it were a

small city of the Midlands.   The special
conditions of the London poor are probably
more like those of Birmingham or some other
Midland town than those of the North.   This
is the solitary London letter sent in.   It is from
Mr. G. Carpenter (aged 69), who says : "As
a boy in this parish (Homerton) I well remember the early forties.   I used to fetch the 4-lb.
loaves of bread for my grandparents.   The
price was elevenpence halfpenny the 4-lb. loaf.
Yesterday I saw at a bakers in the Chatsworth
Road bread 4½d."

Mrs. Margaret Evans, Llamaes House,
Llantwit-Major, Glamorgan, from whom we
gather by correspondence that Mr. William
Shorthouse lived near Birmingham, says :—

"My contribution to the recollections will
be very meagre, but it will be a narrative of
facts.   Joseph Pugh was servant for 50 or 60
years to my grandfather, William Shorthouse,
and at his death, to my grandmother.   My
grandparents both kept excellent accounts, but
alas ! the books have been destroyed.   However, I often put out the men's wages on a
Saturday morning.   Joseph Pugh had 10/- a

week.   He had a large family, and they were unhealthy.   I believe buttermilk was given them, and my grandmother, who could not bear to see the children die one after another, relieved them from time to time with clothing. *Joseph Pugh's wife and daughters used to go early into the meadows and eat snails.*   Herb tea was in ordinary use, as tea, as we understand the word, was 5/- to 10/- per lb. Joseph Pugh was at work before 5 a.m., and left at 6 p.m.   There were no holidays, but on occasions the men left early to go to some village fair.   I used to hear Joseph Pugh churning before 6 a.m., the women servants helping.   Very few of the children of the peasantry of Worcestershire had shoes, and those they had were in holes.

"My recollections begin about 1836, and the figures I have given would hold good till about 1847 or 8.   Wages did not rise very materially till after Joseph Arch's agitation.   Joseph Pugh's wages were raised before Joseph Arch's time—long before—but I do not believe he ever had more than 12/- a week."

PROTECTION IN EAST ANGLIA

CHAPTER II

THE letters naturally emphasise the condition of child-life under Protection, for it is as children that our writers felt its evils. Rook-scaring is, of course, still a common employment of children, but compulsory education has prevented the employment of those as young as Mr. Tiddyment, at the time to which he alludes in our next letter. Comparatively short as it is, it throws a side-light on the rural tyranny as well as poverty of the time :—

"I remember distinctly before I was eight years old having to spend the bitter cold winter days in a large field scaring rooks, and as fast as my little legs could drag over the heavy clay field to one side, the rooks were on the other side ; and many a bitter tear I shed over my failure to scare them. I was brought up on a farm not far from Stanfield Hall, Norfolk. My father was a ploughman, and his wages seven shillings per week, a wife and three children to keep and pay rent. My mother used to go to the fields to glean, as she had a perfect right to do, to keep us alive ; and one day when thus engaged, the steward (the farmer's nephew) came riding into the field, and brutally beat my mother with his riding-whip, and shouted her out of the field. And here I must say when I got a big chap I would have liked to have met that steward and his whip. You would never guess the dainties my father's seven shillings provided for us, and it has been the mystery of my life how my mother eked it out. I have a very distinct recollection of dumplings made of barley meal, and it was with some difficulty I got my teeth through them. Then we had some potatoes, and sometimes we found a swede in the road, having fell off the farm cart. That was a treat indeed! This was our usual weekday fare. But Sunday came, and with something extra for dinner. Meat? Oh no! A simple herring between five of us constituted our Sunday dinner, and the tail, I remember, was my share as a rule. Ah! and then we had tea —sugar we hardly knew the taste of. This tea was such a lovely brown colour; and one day, being rather curious, I thought I would find out what it was made of, and, looking into the teapot, I found some burnt crusts of bread. This was our lot of semi-starvation and slavery. Is it any wonder my father made his escape to that goal of every countryman—London? Here he obtained a situation which he held for thirty years—that is to say, as long as he was able to work. Having made my own way in the world, I have paid just three times the money my father received for the same kind of work on a farm in this county of Surrey. I am nearing the allotted span now, but I retain the remembrance of some of the men who worked on the same farm as myself. One, whose name was Whiting, had a large family. He walked three or four miles night and morning to work. One day I was rather inquisitive as to what he had for dinner, and, boy-like, I inquired. He said, 'Ah, boy! hot dinner to-day.' Having seen no dinner brought, nor any signs of fire anywhere, I had to wait, and presently out of his bag came a piece of dry crust and a good-sized onion. This was all the 'hot dinner' consisted of, and I learned afterwards that this dinner was varied some days by a good-sized apple. Another case I remember, was a man named Cooper. He had a large and young family. The eldest boy used to work with his father, their united wages being sixteen shillings. They earned this extra by land drainage piece work; and it will hardly be believed at this time that the bread bill came to fifteen shillings and four-pence weekly. They paid no rent, as the landlord gave them a cottage by a wood, on condition that his rabbits were protected from the poachers. These things will scarcely be believed in this twentieth century; but I can give the names of every farm where these things occurred, the name of every farmer, and the great landlords of the same; for these things were early engrained into my being. And these are the conditions that our rulers are moving heaven and earth to bring about again!"

The amount of evidence available from the counties of Norfolk and Suffolk is abundant. Very interesting is a communication from the Rev. A. Barnard, a Congregational minister, from which we take the following graphic details :—

"The weekly wages paid to agricultural labourers in that day [*circa* 1840] were about eight shillings in ordinary times, with something extra for the hay and harvest. The question which determined the rate of wages was not what the work done was worth, but what amount a man and his family could subsist on ; not what a man earned, but how many he had to keep. Often the wage received was not enough to buy bread for the family, and so a resort to the purchase of coarser stuff was necessitated to obtain more bulk to meet the wants and stay the cravings of hard-working, hungry men and growing children, such as barley meal, toppings, grey peas, potatoes, and swede turnips. A poor old labourer said to me one Monday, 'I had fine fare yesterday. I had roast, baked, and boiled.' 'Indeed,' said I, 'you were in luck. What did you have? Explain.' 'Well,' said he, 'I and my family had swede turnips, and nothing but swede turnips; but we thought we would have as much variety as we could, so we had roasted turnips, and baked turnips, and boiled turnips.'

"But when flour was at the dearest it was impossible, where there was a large family, for the parents by any expedients to procure a sufficiency of food. Questioning one day a good old man, who had been the father of a large family, and had been very hard hit in those 'good old times,' he said,

'Sir, I remember I had to work all one winter for eight shillings a week. I had a wife and six children to keep out of it, and flour was twelve shillings a bushel. I could take nothing with me but a bare crust, and not enough of that, and then left my family at home, some days, almost foodless. Oh, sir, they were awful times.' And this poor man's wife, in her distress and distraction, said to him, 'Oh, Isaac, what shall we do? Bread is three-halfpence a mouthful!' The best to do could take nothing with them but an onion with their crusts. To be able to get a red herring, and that to be shared by several, was counted a treat. What added to the wickedness of this state of things was that there was no need for it. One farmer candidly said to one of his men who was being cruelly pressed, 'Joe, I could afford to pay you more, but I must not, or the other farmers would be down on me.'

"Sometimes, too, after a wet or bad harvest, for example, the flour would not make bread at all; and the poor people had to make the stuff into 'peel' or 'griddle' cakes, that is cakes made without yeast, 'flected' out, and quickly baked on a 'peel' or 'griddle' over the fire; for when they attempted to make it into loaves, to bake in an oven, only an outside crust could be obtained of a firm consistency, the inside mass remained or became soft and pappy, and would, if thrown on a wall, bespatter it and stick like mud. A really good piece of bread, such as we now get always in abundance, was then a luxury and treat to the poor—greater than roast beef is to-day. As for meat, there were thousands of cottages into which a piece of fresh meat never entered during the year, and only occasionally, in small quantities, a bit of bacon or salt pork. I am speaking of the agricultural villages of the eastern counties; but the state of things in the Midlands seems to have been very much the same. In proof of this I copy from the *Leisure Hour* on the 'good old times': 'There is now living at Epperstone a blind man. He says, " When he was a child *white bread* was considered a great luxury—so much so that when his father used to take his work to Nottingham, he would frequently promise to bring the children a penny white loaf on his return, and such was the eagerness of the little ones to possess this luxury, that they many times went three or four miles to meet their father that they might have it a little sooner, and this, too, in the depth of winter, in frost and snow." '

" Many a mother, to appease the hunger and stop the crying of her children, made bran dumplings. A woman told me that her husband had gone many times to threshing without a bit of bread, and was obliged to relieve the gnawings of hunger by eating some of the pig pease and horse beans he was threshing. If these failed, he was wont to buckle the strap he wore round his loins a hole tighter. Everything in social and national life was arranged in favour of the rich against the poor, on the side of the master against his men. There was one law for the rich and another for the poor. It was lawful for the farmers to combine, but a crime for their men to do so. The labourers had really no constitutional rights, no vote, and no voice in anything, and no privileges and power of any kind. They were too ignorant and weak to proclaim their grievances and wrongs, and there was no press in those days to publish the state of things on the housetops and to whisper it in the ears of a sympathising public. Nobody seemed to care a straw about them. The avowed farmer's ideal of an agricultural labourer was one 'strong in the arm and weak in the head.' "

Mr. Barnard is very decided about two things—the demoralising effect of the state of things obtaining under Protection on both farmers and labourers, and the tendency of monopoly to encourage bad farming. His description of the village life shows Hooligan-ism, now confined to the slum areas of the large cities, prevalent in rural East Anglia. He says : "The character of the sports and amusements of the people was very sottish and brutish. Boxing and wrestling, dog-fighting, cock-fighting, badger-drawing, and other barbarous sports were their delight. Hardly a week passed without a stern and tough 'set-to' between young pugilists; and occasionally two or three quickly followed each other, each growing out of the one that went before. Many of these contests took place in village churchyards, over the graves of the dead. To fight and win was the great ambition of many young men, and wonderfully proud they were of their achievements, and a victorious bruiser was held in great esteem and adored by his fellows. A fight in general was a very relishable show. No attempts were made to stop it, but every encouragement given the combatants to be 'game,' and continue pegging away, till one dropped from sheer exhaustion or something worse.

"Sometimes the whole village of young men would pit themselves against those of another village, and create a civil war on a small scale, after the fashion of the gangs of young roughs which infest the lower parts of London

7

and other great towns at the present time. Animosities were engendered on both sides, and grudges were cherished on a parochial scale, so that it was unsafe for one or two young men to cross into the enemy's camp. They were sure to be set upon and beaten."

This state of things was, no doubt, a survival of primitive manners. Protection did not create such disorders, though the poverty and despair induced by it may have delayed the dying out of barbarism. Mr. Barnard is more directly to the point for us when he shows the tendency of Protection to prevent progress in agriculture. " Let us see," he says, "what kind of farmers they were in the 'good old times.' First, how did they treat their fields ? Many of them were very wretched tillers of the soil. Protection had destroyed the spirit of enterprise, and taken away necessity, one of the strongest stimulants to industry. The less they grew the better price they made of it, and to grow little was less trouble and expense than to grow much. In many cases they only cultivated a portion of the field—the middle part—while acres of waste were left untouched by spade or plough, in the form of wide borders and large corners, overrun with weeds and bushes, and thickly studded with pollard trees, the haunts of game and small birds. I well remember with what delight I, as a child, used to ramble about these uncultivated rings of fields in search of birds' nests and wild-flowers, or where 'hide and seek' and other games were played. Other large spaces were given up to rushes and morass. Great ponds of stagnant water superabounded, and even the cultivated portion was not half drained. This condition of things was to be seen anywhere in the Eastern Counties.

" The system of farming was crop and fallow, and often the preparation for the seed was only a poor apology for cultivation, not half done as compared with the present-day style of farming. One old farmer, I can remember, who lived near my childhood's home, a notoriously profane old man. He had such a curious love for the fitness of things that when he was in a bad temper he clothed himself in shabby clothes, with a special preference for a battered hat.   So when his labourers saw him with this old hat on, they said to each other, ' Here comes old Billy with his swearing hat on.   Look out ! we shall catch it now.' This man was a petty tyrant to all he had to do with—to his men, his household, his cattle, his fields, and himself. One day he began to sow a field with peas.   The soil was so utterly unprepared that one of his men remonstrated with him, telling him that land in such a state never could produce anything.   ' D—— your eyes ! never mind,' was the reply, ' I don't care if they twin. Two for one will pay.' No wonder corn was scarce and starvation always at the door, with the foreign corn shut out, and the home-grown so insufficient and precarious.

" Free Trade, however, revolutionised farming methods. Worthy and capable farmers saw that their salvation lay in better farming, and that abundance must compensate for the loss of high prices.   They earnestly set themselves

to make the land yield her full measure of
increase. They broke up the fallow grounds,
reclaimed the waste places, stubbed the wide
hedgerows and the surrounding briars and
bushes. They burned into useful ashes the
refuse and the weed-choked soil."

We may conclude our notices from Mr.
Bernard's manuscript by giving the following
invoice of food-stuffs for a children's Sunday-
school treat in Protection times :—

	£	s.	d.
Two pecks fine flour, @ 6s.	0	12	0
6 lbs. currants, @ 1s.	0	6	0
6 lbs. sugar @ 8d.	0	4	0
1 lb. caraway seeds @ 1s....	0	1	0
Salt and barm	0	0	6
	£1	3	6

The writer of the next letter is not quite
so old as most of our correspondents, but his
account of Suffolk life just after the Repeal
of the Corn Laws is interesting. We have
kept to our custom of altering the letter in
no way ; but it will readily be seen by the

reader that though the writer shows the defects of his early education he is evidently a very thoughtful man.

" I see from Rynoles's newspaper you solicit corespondence from persons who may have suffered under Protection in England. Although I cannot from personal experience discribe the condition of the poor previous to the Repeal of the Corn Laws, as I was born in that eventfull year, 1844, I con tell you my condition befor the benificial effects of Free Trade had time to devolope. My farther was an agricultural labaurer in the parish of Icklingham, in the county of Suffolk. My grandfarther, who was a widouer, lived with us ; almost a providential circumstance, as the sequence will show. I was the thrid child born out of a family of seven. My grand-fathr was born in the year 1780 ; he commenced work when seven years of age, and ceased working for wages in 1854, and althow capable of doing all kinds of farm work with cridit to himself and his emplorer (except during harvest) his wages never exceeded

eight shillings per week, and for many years
of his married life his wages were seven
shillings per week ; and I have heard him
relate the terriable condition of himself and
other in the village befor I was born. Barley
bread was the stapel articul of food. My
father was born in 1814, and commenced work
with his father at 8 years of age, who was
a shepard for the esqure in the village. When
in his teens he commenced general farm work,
and his wage never rose higher than seven
shillings per week till 1840, when he wooed
and won my mother, than he obtained the
extra shilling per week alowed to married
men. With this magnificent sum my mother
commenced housekeeping, out of which she
was expected to find food, clothing, firing,
and rent. As I was the thrid child boorn
(in 1844) I con quit see her dificulties would
soon begin. My first vived recollection of
hunger commenced in Febuary. On returning
from school with my eldest sister, we found
the door of our cottage locked, and although
we could not understand what was going on

inside the house, we could hear some one in, and we stood crying and knocking at the door, till a neighbour opened the door and bid us to brush off to school again.   My sister, who had evidently done the same thing before, took me on to the cabbage bed and puled up some of the cabbage stalks, from which the cabbages and been cut, and peeled of the outer rine, and the centre we eate for our dinner, and many times after we did the same thing.   On returnig hom at night we learned another littel sister had been found under the gooesberry bush, and by this I am enabled to fix the date as Febuary, 1849.   In October, 1852, I resolved to seek a job, and, keeping my intentions to myself, I visited all the farmers in the village without sucess ; no doubt from my diminitive statue and pinched looks they would conclude my sirvesus were not worth the current wage for starters, namely, one shilling per week.   But on my way back home I saw two men taken up carrots for the village miller, and stoping to look at them I said ' Won't the tops have to be cut off befor they are carred home?' and one of the men replied, 'Yes.'

"I out with my pocket-knife at once and commenced opperations, which seemed to be fun for the two men. When the miller came some time after he greeted me with, 'Halo, boy, who set you on?' When one of the men said 'Why, he set hisself on,' to which the miller added, 'Go on, my boy; one volinteer is worth ten press men.' On the Saturday night I called at his house for my pay. He was a stout, gruff man, and he shouted, 'How many days have you been my boy?' I told him. 'And how much a day do you want?' I replied '2d.,' as I knew that was the regular price for boys starting to work. Looking steadly at me he said, 'And what made you commence to work without been set on?' I commenced to cry, and said I wanted to help mother. This evidently tuched his pocket as well as his heart, as he arose from his seat and patted me on the head, and said, 'Don't cry, my boy; you have don nothing wrong. As you have worked so well I shall give you 3d. a day,' and, handing me the coin, said, ' Now take that home to your mother, and keep a good boy, than you will grow a good man.' On arriveing home I showed my sisters my erenings; they danced for joy, and father segested we should have a good super for once, as this was my first pay. My oldest sister was at once sent of to the village shope for a pound of salt pork; with that and some boiled potatoes we regaled ourselves, and peace and happiness reigned in the household. With the winter intervening (1853) my father's wage, than 9s. per week, was the only suport we had for 5 sisters, myself, and father and mother, till the following summer, when the Esq. wife sought my servicous to look after her turkeys at the splendard renumation of one shilling per week of seven days; and here let me add, once for all, that these wages were not suplemented by food or any other priviledges. How to exist and keep honist was the mistrey that confrunted my parents; final result, it could not be done. My father, therefor, like otheres in the same perdicament, brought home from the farm potatoes, turnips, carrots, &c., in fact anything that was eatiable. But our condition up to this time was louxerous compared to what we suffered in the winter of 1854 and '55, when bread rose to famine prices. I supose for fear the whole villagers died from starvation, the Esq. rose the wages up to 12s. per week, and this was the high-water mark for wages in Suffolk till Joseph Arch formed the Labourers' Union. With the close of the Rusain War wages droped back to 1s. 6d. per day, as before. The winter of 1854 and '55 was the worst time that I remember; my father had 20 roods of alot-ment ground, for which he paid to the Esq. 10s. per annum, but through the insufficency of manure and constantly been croped with potatoes, they often proved a failir. So to give the land a change he decided to plant it with parsnips, intending to sell the parsnips and buy potatoes with the money. Poor man! he never seemed to have asked himself the question, ' Who could buy them ? ' The result was they could be neither sold or exchanged

for potatoes ; we had, therefor, to eate them ;
and, to add to our missery, owing to bad
weather my father lost a great deal of work,
so with scarcely any bread we practily lived on
parnsnips—if fact, like Daniel's prayers, they
came 3 times a day. After the harvest of
1855 my father obtained work at the gravel
pits, riddeling stones for the roads. The
working of this gravel was let by the Esq.
to a contractor, who emploied the men ; as
this was peice work, the men sometimes made
11s. or 12s. per week. With this prospect in
view we entered the winter of 1856 with bright
prospects, till one Saturday night, just into the
new year, when my father handed mother his
week's wages he told her there was no more
work at the gravel pits, as Bobey (the Esq.)
had stoped the work. This news brought
consternation into our littel camp, for this
arbitary conduct on the part of the Esq., we
afterwards learned, was because some of the
gravel workers had been boasting at the
village pub. that they were indipendent of
Bobey and his farms. When this got to his

ears he at once gave orders that no more gravel had to be won. Of cours my father had to suffer with the reste. He now tramped from farm to farm, but no work could be obtained. Maddend by his non-sucess, he arrived home one evening and declared he would take us all to the workhouse. This declaration raised my mother's temper, and she said 'Never!' we would all die rather than go their. In vain he pleaded with her, and, young as I was, I put in my word, and said 'Mother, Bill Capp said he got plenty of bread when he was in; let us go!' This brought tears all round. My grandfather, who through old age and infirmity was receveing four shillings a week from a friendly society, said 'No,' we should not go to the workhouse; we should share with him. My father, dispareing of perswading my mother to take us to the workhouse, declared he would run away and leave us, as he could not stop and hear us crying for bread; and, poor fellow! he did go, we knew not wither. In fortnight's time he returned, all smiles; he had suceeded in obtaining work in the neighbourhood of Ely, and by ruffing it in both lodging and food he was able to bring home a few shillings to mother.

"Such, sir, were the conditions in which we lived in my young days, and there was littel, if any, improvement till I would endure it no longer, and in 1863, although only a small ladie, not more than 7 stone in weight, I left the dear old clay house and determond to fight life's battel under better conditions, if such were to be found.   In conclusion, sir, I can safely say dureing the first 18 years of my life my belley had not been properly filled 18 time since I was weaned from my mother's breast.   Scores and scores of times have I sat under the hedghrows and cried, and told God how good I would be if He only sent me bread.   I had not then learned that God only help those who help themselves.   Perhaps some will think my case was an exceptionaly one.   To such I might say, 'No, by no means ; ours was better than many, as my father alwas brought his wages home, wereas some of the

men spent part of theirs at the village pub.'
Now, sir, should you think well to publish
the above, and they should be read by any
who are asked by Mr. Chamberland to vote
for Protection, to such I would say let their
reply be ' Let us have all commodities free
from taxes, *but protect the people.*'—I am, sir,
yours respectfully,

"EDWARD COOK."

G. Ruffel, The Avenue, Brightlingsea,
Essex, sends a shrewd letter : " I am a
native of Suffolk, and born September 7,
1816, at farmhouse previously held by my
grandfather, under Squire Jennings, at a rent
of 5/- per acre.   At grandfather's death, Uncle
John took it, and died there.   About that
time Esqr. Jennings died, and the estate fell
into the hands of an earl, who employed a
sharp agent, and he raised the rents to 25/-
per acre when my father took it, as there had
been great improvements made by father and
son, and the protective duty on corn, &c., existed.

" At that time wheat was about 10/- per
bushel, pork 3d. lb., beef and mutton 3d.

to 4d. per lb., eggs 30 for 1 shilling, butter 7d. lb., cheese 1½d. to 2d. (called 'Suffolk loaf'), men's wages 7/- to 8/- per week, head horsemen 9/-.   My father was tenant to about 1830, and had about £200 worth of hay, which he had to leave without 1d. compensation. (The farm had been in family 100 years.) Father took a farm in Essex, at a time the tythe was 2/6 per acre on the arable land, and nothing on the marshes.   About 1836 the tythe was assessed at 7s. per acre on the arable land, and 3s. 6d. per acre on the marshes (a fine plumb for the parsons).   So much for the Tythe Commutation Act, which was simply a parsons' Act.

"These observations are from my personal experience.   About 1834 I was engaged on surveys of parishes in Mid-Suffolk for tythe commutation, and bread was 1s. 1d. to 1s. 2d. per loaf of 4 lbs., and meat 3d. to 4d. per lb., coal 1s. 3d. per bushel, and but little wood for the labourers, wages 6s. per week for single men, and 7s. to 7s. 6d. do. for married men, head horsemen 9s. per week.

I told the farmers it was a parsons' Act, and
he had six days out of the seven to study how
he could best them, and they would not see
it.   I told them the parson could get from
the men or their wives the quantity of corn
they grew, and the papers would give them
the price, and they would lay a balance-sheet
before them, with labour a small item.   I tried
to advise them to pay their men £1 per week
at once, before the assessment was made, as
the men would spend 19s. per week for their
produce, and benefit both.   If not, they would
have to pay three times more tythe than
before, and the landlord, seeing this, would
want more rent, but they would not hearken.
There would be these *two* to contend with,
and the third would come if the labourers got a
little education.   They would tell you they
could get more wages anywhere than you was
paying them, and your answer must be, ' The
parson have emptied one pocket and the landlord the other, and left nothing for you, so
you must go, and half the land will go out
of cultivation.'

8

" About 1840 I paid a visit to an uncle at Dalham, Suffolk, who told me he had been talking with Sir James Affleck, of the Hall. Affleck said : ' All us masters will be ruined. They are going to take the duty off wool, which sells at 2s. 6d. per lb., and will come down to 1s. 3d. if done.'

" *Ruffell.*   ' And a good thing too !   Look at the price of mutton ; and if these poor men could get to work and had money, mutton would be 6d. per lb. directly.

" *Affleck.*   ' I had not seen it in that light before, and will vote for the duty to come off.'

" *Ruffell.*   ' We have both our stores full of wool, and can only sell a few fleeces occasionally ; and I should be pleased to clear mine out at 1s. 3d. per lb.   It would be a great boon to the distressed manufacturers and their men.' "

The Free Traders of Norfolk recently collected into an interesting pamphlet, the results of interviews with several old residents in the County.   East Anglia being a purely rural district, with little demand for labour outside farming, the condition of the agricultural labourer has always been exceptionally hard. That in the days of Protection it was terrible is a fact of which these interviews give ample evidence.

The first is with Mr. Harry Banham, of Caston, described as "a typical son of the soil." He has lived in the village of Caston all his life, and married when he was twenty-one years old. He was then an agricultural labourer. His wife had seven children. He left the land to work in the mill.

"For years," said Mr. Banham, "I never knew the colour of money. I worked in the mill, and was allowed a certain amount of flour each month in lieu of wages, and even then I did not get enough flour to meet the wants of my hungry family. I got into debt with the miller, but when my children grew up we were able to pay him everything. My wife, in spite of her big family, was forced to work in order to get a few of the necessities of life. Two or three times a week she used to fetch coal from Attleborough in a little donkey-cart, and by this means earned 4s. or 5s. a week. Meat in those days was the greatest luxury. Flour was 3s. a stone." According to Mrs. Banham " The young people have no idea what a terrible struggle we had then. We worked night and day just for existence. We depended upon harvest for rent money, and my husband has worked from the first break of day until dark mowing hay. Then we women used to sow the corn, but it was dreadfully hard work pegging away all day with bended backs. I would rather stand at the wash-tub all day long than do that work again. It was terrible. As the children grew up the burden lightened, and food began to get cheaper, the price of flour was reduced, and we began to get along better. If they raise the price of food again the larger labouring class families cannot possibly be properly fed. Where there are larger families now it takes them all their time. The old folks nowadays don't know what we old folks had to go through when we were young. They live pretty comfortably compared with the old times, and the labourers daughters dress quite as well as the farmer's wives did years ago. You couldn't tell a farmer of those days from a labourer of to-day, although he got a bigger price for his wheat. I can remember when flour was 4s. 3d. a stone, and when the commonest sugar, which we now get for 1½d., was 7d. a lb. I have known times when I have scarcely dared to pick up a loaf of bread for fear of cutting it up too quickly. Men used to wait until night to go and steal turnips with which to feed their children. But we never could do that. Life was a fearful thing in those days—we never knew what pleasure was then!"

Mrs. Fisher, of Scoulton, an old lady of eighty-eight years, but of remarkably alert intelligence, said to the interviewers: "I remember the time when labourers only got 9s. a week, when flour was 3s., and at one time 4s. a stone, when poor people lived on swedes and turnips, which they stole from the fields. I have heard my mother say that at one time, when pork was 11s. a stone, it cost another 5s. to salt the pig down. Boys who now get

5s. and 6s. a week for crow-scaring would only get 9d. for a whole week in those days. Labouring men could only get half an ounce of tea a week then, now they buy at least a quarter of a pound. Why talk about those days being better that these? Don't tell me about them! They were terrible."

The interviewers got much valuable information from Mr. George Mimms, a Guardian, of Walton. He is in his eighty-sixth year. "I was one of thirteen children," he said, "and my father farmed about 100 acres of land. As a little farmer my father was hard up—immensely so in bringing up such a large family. We lived extremely hard, and as boys we used to sing the old rhyme—

   "'Barley cake as black as hake,
     Without a mite of butter for the barley cake.'

"If my father had a wish for a piece of white bread, my mother had to sift the bran from the meal and make white flour. We thought as much of getting a piece of white bread in those days as a poor man now does of getting a piece of cake. As to the poor men, they were poor indeed. I remember my father, with his little farm, was so troubled about his men, who had nothing to do, that he used to have acres of land dug by the spade to find work for the men. Shiploads of men were sent to America because there was nothing for them to do in rural England. Two of my brothers went to America because my father did not know what to do with them. The labourer's life was cruel. They were little more than serfs. A single labourer got 1s. a day, and a man with a family 9s. or 10s. a week. Flour was 2s. 6d. a stone, and more in the times of war. They were tremendous days. There were very, very poor people then. I have known men by chance get a little piece of bacon, and that was all. There is a tremendous difference between the scanty spread of the labourer's table in my boyhood and the provisions in a labourer's home to-day. Everything was dear when I was young. To take the town of Walton, I should say there was ten times less spent than now. Walton then possessed about two little shops, now it is a thriving little commercial town with excellent shops, and it served the same district then as it does now. Our workhouses then were gross. I have been a guardian for upwards of thirty years, and I know the poor people are provided for a thousand times better now than they were in the dark days. In the old times I have known a red herring to be divided amongst three persons, who thought it was a lucky thing to get that."

From the same authority we learn that Mr. Mark Moore, of Great Cremingham, a man apparently of eighty years of age, affirmed that : "The labouring classes did not live in those days—theirs was only a bare existence. Where there was a family the deficiency of income had to be supplied by parish relief. Of course bread was exceedingly dear. The staple food of the people was rye bread. Sometimes that was none too good, especially after a wet harvest. Then when the people put their bread into a basin of milk it would sink to the bottom like lead. I have known rye bread to be so doughy that the knife with which it was cut had to be cleaned at each slice taken. Sometimes it was so bad that they had to make little cakes of it. In this village the labouring classes half lived on swedes. The children used to have swedes for break-fast. They were really half-starved in the days of Protection. The people wore the coarsest of clothing made of strong materials. The women were very smart if they had an orange and blue cotton dress. That would not suit the young people now. The people did not really know anything about tea then —tea-drinking was out of the question. It was too dear. Sugar was 8d. lb., and the coarsest was 7d. It is the duty of those of my generation to tell the present generation that during the days of Protection the country suffered terribly, and destitution was rife among the poor. Not even at the bidding of Mr. Chamberlain must we submit again to the taxation of the staple foods of the people."

A very striking old couple, Mr. and Mrs. John Wilkins, of Northwold, gave an interesting account of their early struggles. The husband said : " I only earned 6s. a week when I was as good a man as ever laboured. That was in the days of dear food. I worked for 7s. a week when I was married and had got two children." Mrs. Wilkins, who is seventy-five, and her husband eighty-three, tells us : " My husband used to bring $\frac{1}{2}$ lb. of pork home for Sundays, and I have seen him divide it up amongst his children and not take a piece for himself. He would eat bread and onions, and not make a word over it. I have known him take out bread in the morning and bring it home again at night so that his fellow-workmen should not see he was unable to get any. My children I have had to put supperless to bed many and many a time. We could not get enough food. They were dreadful times. I cannot tell you how we clothed our children. I have collected sticks and made a fire, bought a half-pennyworth of soap and washed the children's clothes on Saturday night and dried them ready for Sunday morning. Now the young people dress like ladies. In the old days farmers went to church in 'slops.' A young labourer wouldn't even go like that now—he must have his Sunday clothes. Ah! times have altered. A little child now knows as much as we old folks. We had no schooling. We have had experience, though, and may God never permit them to go through the same." According to Mr. Wilkins, in his young days "We used to have rye bread. If you cut the crust off and threw the remainder at the wall it would stick there. Then we used to have sharps, which seemed to burn inside after we had eaten it. It was awful stuff. The pigs have it now. It is a shame to think of taxing the poor man's bread. Let him have a bellyful of bread, if nothing else. There were no drawing-rooms and no finery at farmhouses then."

From other interviews we gather various matters. Mr. and Mrs. Abraham, of Denver, "could only buy $\frac{1}{2}$ oz. of tea and half a pound of sugar a week; they could not get anything

but bread to eat, and not enough of that."
Mrs. Mary Pell "had to boil rice and peas to
mix with the flour to make sufficient bread,
when her family was small." Another old lady
remembered when she made "tea" of burnt
crusts of bread. "They were really always in a
state of hunger; they lived, and that was all."
"When I got married," says one witness,
"my wages were 7s. 6d., and flour was 3s. a
stone; and I worked from four till eight."
Another had seen the children "run like pigs
after an apple-core in the streets." "In the
old days," says one lady, "of dear food, the
women and girls had to turn out into the fields
and work laboriously to make up the in-
sufficiency in their family income. Really the
poor people were half starved; *they never
knew what it was not to be hungry.*" Mr.
George Crowfoot, of Ashill, told the inter-
viewer the following anecdote: "I remember
on one occasion I had no bread to take with
me to work, and when the other men sat
down to eat what they had got for dinner, I
found I had a little tobacco dust in my pipe.

I looked about to see if master was near, and
thought all was right ; so I lit my pipe to try
and drive the hungry feeling away.   Before a
minute was up a shout came over the hedge,
' Who's that smoking ? '   We all denied
smoking, because they would not permit it
on the farms.   I owned up afterwards, and
had to suffer for it.   He gave me three days'
holiday.   Ah! I can remember when my wife
bought half a pound of bacon and made
dumplings for the children, and rather than
they should not have all, she has gone without.
The people were half starved then."   Another
witness, who earned 9s. a week when flour
was 4s. a stone, tells us that in those days
"farmers went about in smock-frocks."   John
Coggles, of Swaffham, said that a labourer
who wore a blue "slop" and a new handkerchief round his neck, soon became the beau of
the village.   He had seen a halfpenny herring
divided between four persons!   Many state
that bread and onions was their most ordinary
dinner.   For gravy one had the water in
which dumplings had been boiled, with a little

flour to thicken it. " The people," says one, " were almost starved into rebellion."

We will only give one more extract from this helpful collection of reminiscences. "Mr. William Smith, of Holme Hale, said : ' When I was a young man I got 5s. 6d., 4s. 6d., and sometimes only 4s. a week. Married men got 1s. 6d. extra, so I, like a good many more, was silly enough to get married in order to get the 1s. 6d. I got married on a Sunday so I should not lose any time, but when I went to work next morning my master said he didn't want me ; as a matter of fact he didn't want to give me the 1s. 6d. extra. He afterwards took me on again. When my wife was ill the parish paid for the nurse. It was impossible to have a doctor ; I had no money to pay him; we absolutely had to depend on parish relief when illness came. I can remember before I was married flour was 4s. a stone ; that was just before Free Trade was proclaimed—in the early forties. What did we eat with our bread ? Why, sometimes an onion, sometimes none. I have known as many as sixteen men running about the village playing marbles simply because they had got nothing to do, and the farmers did not want them. What was the reason why they would not employ the men, do you ask? Why, because the rent of the land was so high. The price of fairly good soil in the old days was £2 an acre to the farmer, and then he had to pay the tithe and rates and taxes, and find the labour and horses and implements. They got an extra price for their corn, but I reckon they were far worse off than they are now. There is land in this parish that used to let at £2 an acre and tithe, now lets at 7s. 6d., tithe free. But I must tell you this story; it is true. A woman bought a pound of pork, out of which she made fourteen flour-and-water dumplings on consecutive days, and served two slices for Sunday dinner. She was indeed a clever woman! It was something even to get the flavour of sausage in those days. Tea was then 4½d. an oz., and brown coarse sugar 4d. We never had jam, and we used to look upon rice as a luxury. Eggs were cheaper then, and herrings were good, but we had no money to buy them.   Coal was 9d. a bushel, but we used to burn turf.   We used oat flights for beds.   We used blankets when we were fortunate enough to get them given us by the parish."

PROTECTION IN SOUTH-EASTERN ENGLAND

CHAPTER III

PROTECTION IN SOUTH-EASTERN ENGLAND

THE letters from South-eastern England are of a specially depressing character, owing perhaps to the purely agricultural nature of the country. We could have wished for more evidence as to the condition of the people in the hop-country when David Copperfield trudged through it to Dover ; but Kent says little. Perhaps in the immediate neighbourhood of the London labour market things may have been slightly better than in most parts of the county. But, if better, they can have been only slightly so : for even in London wages were low, and it was even less easy to find turnips and other substitutes for bread than farther afield. It will be seen that one of our letters refers to both the counties of Hants and Wilts. Wiltshire does not of course belong to this chapter, but we have kept this particular letter among the others containing Hampshire evidence.

"L. S." gives us some insight into social conditions and prices in the county of Essex. He says: "In answer to yours in the *Christian World* upon the question of Protection in the bad old times, I can tell you a little. Born in the year 1830, in a country village in Essex, put to work at the age of 9 years—many of the children of the village at work before that—for the pay 1s. per week. No school in the village, only kept by an old dame; no British or National schools at that time; no Sunday Schools, only at the old Meeting, as then called, now the Congregational Church; numbers of children had no learning but what they got there; lads from 12 to 15 years of age learning to spell small words, such as 'I can not see God, but God can see me,' the first lesson after learning the alphabet.

"At the age of 16 years I was put to the

grocery business ; will give you some of the prices I have sold goods at. Bread, 1s. 0½d. per quartern loaf ; tea, 5s. per lb., numbers of the poor could buy but one ounce per week, 4d. ; sugar, 6d. and 6½d. per lb., one year it was 7½ per lb. ; loaf sugar, 9d.; currants, 10d.; cotton and rush candles, 8d. ; soap, 6d. ; pepper, 2 oz. [" L. S." omits here to fill in the price] ; rice, 4d. and 6d. ; butter, 8d. to 1s. ; coals, 1s. 8d. per cwt. ; these are only a few things. Labourers' wages, from 9s. to 11s. per week. Well, there was families had but little besides a piece of bread ; at night their supper a few hot potatoes, little salt, and bread. Perhaps they might manage to get one pound of pork for the week. That was a treat. Many of the poor had to buy ' toppings,' could not afford flour. Most of the women went into the fields to work in the summer for the sum of 8d. or 10d. per day. They were glad for the little boys and girls, 7 or 8 years old, to go to work to bring in a little. The money the men got for harvest, and the women had their gleaning corn, had to go for rent and a few clothes. A good domestic servant's wages, five or six pounds per year, was considered very high.

"From 1846–1872 I was in the grocery trade, and have seen some painful cases of want. I hope never to see Protection again. It is difficult now to make the young people understand it—if it comes they will be worse off than the older generations. The present generation cannot manage as the former one. Every word I have written, sir, is true."

It will be seen that " L. S. " went into the grocery business in the year of repeal. The prices he gives doubtless refer to that year, and those of the bad harvests immediately following.

We do not know in what district Mr. Jordan was living at the time of which he writes, but we include his letter here as he confirms " L. S." Like " L. S." he points out in effect that the poor of the present day, many of them, have not been accustomed to such dire poverty as their grandparents, and that this unfits them for resuming a struggle which the latter managed to carry on somehow.

"94, MORTON ROAD, W.,
"18/2/04.

"SIR,—In the *Christian World* I notice your desire for the experience of those who remember Protection in the forties—which I consider a good idea, and may have an enlightening effect on those who lack the knowledge.

"I can assert that in those times employment was very scarce—uncertain, difficult to obtain and retain, in fact most casual—also badly paid for. Bread was thought cheap at 9d. the 4-lb. loaf, 11d. and 1s. was an ordinary price; 8d. was, I should say, the lowest. The misery of those time I remember most keenly, and do hope the people of these times will not return to them; for my firm conviction is, that after so glad a time of Free Trade, a return would cause national trouble—the change would cause such discontent—the people having tasted the sweets, which was not the case formerly.—I am, yours truly, "G. JORDAN."

Mrs. Lucy Buckland, Clarence Villa, Hawlee Court Road, Westcliffe-on-Sea, Essex, writes: "I had the enclosed cutting given to me yesterday, and on reading it, decided to send you a few lines in reference to the 'Chamberlain policy.' I certainly can do more in point of fact than he can, being twenty years his senior, and so being able to speak from my own personal experience, which, before the hated corn laws were repealed, was bad indeed. In reference to ordinary living, groceries of all kinds were double the price than at the present time. I had a young family, and had to pay 11d. per loaf for bread— which, by the way, was any weight the baker liked to give. From the time that Free Trade was established, the price of all necessary things came down, making a way for poor people to have many things which previously it was not possible for them to procure. Jam, for instance, owing to the dearness of sugar, was an impossible luxury, being sold in very *small* gally-pots at sixpence each. Tea and sugar *more* than double what they are now, and the

working man's weekly wages on the average [1]
30s. per week. All these miseries for the
toilers have now become so different that to go
back to the former state of things must bring
them to extreme poverty. Asking you to
pardon this intrusion on your time, and to put
the mistakes made in this communication to
my nearly 88 years of age."

Mr. Thomas Mitchell, 80, Gayville Road,
Wandsworth, writes : "As a lad living in the
year 1845–6, at Farnham, Surrey, I well
remember a very wet summer. In consequence the corn was all sprouting, and therefore unfit for food of man, only cattle ; but we
had not then obtained the blessings of a cheap
loaf, the labours of Bright, Cobden, and other
friends of the people not having at that time
been brought to bear on the question of Free
Trade. In the autumn of year named the
said growing corn, when ground in flour, was
purchased by myself and also brother at two

---

[1] Presumably Mrs. Buckland means the average wage of
working men now. This is about correct, for *all trades*,
but is, of course, much higher than was then the case.

shillings and tenpence a peck, for making home-made bread and puddings. This price worked out at one shilling per quartern loaf (oh the good old times of Protection!). I well remember the starvation of those times. Puddings when made with this growing corn flour, when cooked, fell into a mass on the dish, really uneatable. The bread came from the oven in flat cakes. Upon keeping one day, a slice when cut, if pulled apart, was as though cob-webby, the colour then black, and it stank. Now such bread would be condemned as unfit for food; then, there was no remedy, that or none. To make matters worse, the potato crop was a failure. Meat, as a rule, obtainable in small doses; butcher's meat once a week. Of course at that time there was no importa-tion of meat from any quarter, either the alive or frozen, therefore then the masses of poor people in this country were in a bad, desperate, and starving condition. Since the advent of Free Trade our people have lived better in every way—good flour and bread, plenty of meat of every kind to suit every purchaser's pocket, dried fruit of all kinds, apples, oranges, lemons, tea, coffee, all farinaceous foods at half the rate paid in those bad old times. Sugar, best Demerara, now 2½d., those days 6d. Innumerable other things might be quoted, but space fails. All this goes to show that the purchasing power of money is greatly increased, the food obtainable for same money being double to three times. The cottages and homes of the people have also greatly improved from the same causes. And now, after experiencing these advantages all these years, is the valuable education we have gained in these matters to be thrown away upon the advice of an unstable man, who has dangled great prizes before our eyes in the past and failed, and would again if he is entrusted with the chance?"

South-eastern England has been silent compared with other purely agricultural districts. We have, however, several very interesting letters from Hampshire. Hampshire is to a large extent a rural county, and is one which, perhaps, suffered more than its share during the days of the bread tax. It is said that "Nothing that cannot walk should leave a Hampshire farm." This bit of local proverbial philosophy lets us see how much Hampshire would suffer in days when meat was cheap and bread dear. Pasture land was, no doubt, forced into corn bearing, and thus a double violence would be done to nature. We may presume that the land would not yield the same amount of produce obtained in counties better suited to wheat, the farmers would be worse off, and the labourers probably even worse paid. The first of our letters, by a writer who adopts the pseudonym, "A Hampshire Hog," deals not only with his own county but also with the neighbouring county of Wilts.

"So many extraordinary assertions have been made as to the prosperity in our country during the days of Protection, that I may be permitted to give a few unvarnished facts as witnessed by myself. My earliest impression of the unfortunate conditions of the farm labourers commenced about the year 1832, during which the agricultural riots occurred.

The people, resenting the introduction of thrashing machines as likely to reduce their already scanty wages, commenced a raid, and smashed as many implements as they could lay their hands on. With the assistance of the military and yeomanry the disturbances were ended, and there began a series of rick-burnings, varied by an occasional homestead burning.

" Many arrests were made, and severe sentences followed conviction, a few cases of hanging, and many transportations for life—the latter sometimes considered the more terrible. The long passage to Australia, and the treatment afterwards, where little or no supervision was possible, awaited the poor wretches. Of such things the men of to-day have no conception.

" A learned judge, addressing the grand jury at the Winchester Assizes, declared the labouring population was ' vicious to a man,' and implored the country gentlemen to step in and stay the plague. Wages to the ordinary labourer ranging from 7s. to 8s. and 9s., according to the price of wheat; shepherds and head carters usually 1s. above weekly pay, with cottage free, together with Michaelmas money, and fagots for the winter fuel. All this time every article of food and clothing was far above the prices of to-day.

"In the month of February, 1841, I left my village home to be apprenticed to a firm of grocers in a large way of business in Wiltshire, and now I began to understand the privations of the poor. The wages were even a little below Hampshire, and the limited purchases of the country people astonished me, and their abject complaining was distressing to a degree. Women employed in rough field work, such as weeding or pulling turnips, earned 6d. per diem. At piece work the men did a little better. The price paid per acre was, as seen to-day, absurd, and, in fact, many of your readers would not believe it possible for body and soul to be kept together on such a scale.

"There was a surplus of labour, and few outlets beyond the village of their birth. A

few drifted into the towns, and the recruiting
sergeant periodically at fairs selected some of
the best lads.   The girls made excellent
domestic servants, and many farmer's wives
took pains to instruct them for situations, where
higher wages were obtainable.   The village
school teaching in those days was rudimentary
and of short duration.

"The farmers in South Wilts were a fine
race of men, and kindly in disposition for the
most part.   Some abused their power, which
was almost absolute ; and when a farm was
carried on on strictly commercial principles,
devoid of any old associations, the law of
supply and demand was terribly hard on
Hodge.

"In Protection days a bad harvest not only
meant dear bread, but bad bread.   There was
no dry foreign wheat to fall back upon, and we
had to put up with our own.   Sifted barley
meal made into bannocks fell to the lot of
many extremely poor with large families.   Of
course potatoes were largely consumed until
the disease appeared among them.   In

the manufacturing district things were bad. Batches of men, women, and children wandered south in hopeless destitution, and, to use the words of an Oldham manufacturer, 'utter starvation prevailed.'"

Mr. H. Cole, Hayling Island, Hants, writes: "I can tell you of my experience in the 'Hungry Forties,' as you term them, and well I know it. I was born on this island in the year 1834, and can well remember. I can say that I saw wheat ricks standing in the rick-yard when the wheat was at its highest price—at the time I am speaking I think about £30 a load, or thereabout—and the owner would not thresh it out, because he said that was not money enough. Well, them ricks stood there until the outer ears of the rick grew green all round. Then there was a fall in corn, when we got the Free Trade, and it fell, and then the farmer threshed his corn out, and tried to sell it. Some he took to market, and sold at about half the same sum. Some he brought back again, could not sell it for a long time. I can remember bread was 2s. 2d. per gallon loaf, tea

4s. to 5s. per pound, sugar 5d. and 6d. per pound. I know my father used to get a sack of wheat from the farmer, and take it to the mill, and get it ground, and we would bring it home just as it was, without any dressing whatever. Mother used to sieve it, and take out just the roughest of the bran, and then she would bake it for us. Of course we had an oven to bake our own bread, and the wages was low. There was 9 of us in family, and father and mother. As I said, I was born in '34, and one brother older than me, so we were all young. It was hard times. Some poor I knew was glad to get what they termed 'sharps,' and make bread of it. I knew one man acquaintance of mine, with a large family of young girls, a labouring man, and I have known him to walk miles in the morning to his work with only bread to eat. I can vouch for the truth of that, as one of the girls is now my wife, so we both know the pinch of that time ; but we have now been married 42 years, and still in good health, thank God ; but I should not like to see such times again as that was. I think

10

agricultural labourers used to get 10s. to 11s. a week to keep themselves and family."

Here is another pathetic letter which carries the same lesson as all the rest : " I was born in the year of our Lord, 1831. At that time my father was a hand-loom weaver of sail-cloth for the firm of Thompson & Co., of the town of Fordingbridge, Hants. I do not know how much he earned in the shape of wages at that time. He gave the weaving up some three years after I was born, and then went to work in the bleaching department, and his wages was 9s. per week. There was four children, and he paid 1s. 6d. for house rent, so that everything else and the cost of living had to be done out of 7s. 6d. per week, and the price of bread at that time was from tenpence to sixteenpence per gallon loaf ; and I have often known the time when there was not a morsel of food in the house, and had to go to bed hungry ; and I well reckolect some one gave my mother a little barley meal, and she sifted it and took out the coarse parts, and then made it into what was called barley bannicks. As to tea, sugar, and meat wee scarcely saw any. I reckolected mother getting once a pound of bacon for dinner on Sunday; but a pound divided amongst six was not much; and for dinner on week-days at times was potatoes with one pennyworth of suet fried, and the fat poured over the potatoes after being mashed. My mother often cried to think that all she could get for my father's dinner was a penny bloater, and had to work 12 hours a day, and, of course, the children's dinner was only potatoes and salt. But for the whole of the time wee did not have half enough to eat. I had to go very early to work in the bleaching yard, and my wages was one farthing per hour, or threepence per day of 12 hours; and I can assure you that when I think of those times a large lump rises in my throat, and yet to-day there are men doing all they can to bring back those days. If you think, sir, that this will help on the cause of Free Trade and free food, publish it by all means. By so doing you will greatly oblige.—Respectfully yours,

"E. C. Gosney."

Mr. Thomas Barker, Roseleigh, Littlehamp-
ton, Sussex, writes :—

"I was born in June, 1834, in the county of
Bucks, so I am nearing the 70th mile-stone
in the journey of life. I was one of several
children born to my parents within ten years,
my father being a shoemaker. I cannot quote
market prices for wheat, but I can remember
well enough when the quartern loaf for some
considerable time was 1s. 1d., and 1s. 2d. for a
few weeks. At that time we children had two,
by no means thick, slices of bread and lard—it
wouldn't run to butter; and no matter how
keen our appetites these two slices had to
suffice. Yet with this economical, sparing
arrangement, the bread and flour bill for the
week totalled up to close upon 10s.

"I remember well enough hearing it said that
certain farmers, wheat-growers, in that neighbourhood, were keeping their wheat ricks
standing in the farmyard, waiting and hoping
that the long prices then prevailing would
become still longer; and one notable instance
engraved itself into my memory. This was a

case in which a farmer had kept a wheat rick standing so long as to require re-thatching, and when the men got up to the rick they suddenly disappeared, in consequence of the interior of the rick having been eaten away by rats and mice. In this way the avarice of the rick owner was righteously, as I think, requited.

"At the time of which I am writing the farm labourer's wage was 10s. per week for six day work, and 11s. for the cattle men, whose services were required on Sundays. In cases, of which there were many, where the labourer's family was numerous, his wages didn't more than cover his bread and flour bills; and it goes without saying almost, that in very many instances much of the bread and flour had of the bakers was never paid for, and no wonder.

"I can remember the pleasure with which we young folks learned that the Corn Laws had been abolished, and that the days were coming when we might have what we liked off the loaf instead of being 'allowanced,' and made to put up with an insufficient quantity of the 'staff of life.'   I am more than amazed to know there are some, even now, who would like a bread and flour tax reimposed; but they never can have experienced, as we older men have, the rigour and hardship of the Protectionist period, happily of long ago.   Since the times to which my letter pertains, nearly every article of home consumption has cheapened, and no amount of argument from Joseph Chamberlain, with the meek and mild assent of Jesse Collings, will ever shake my faith in and love for 'Free Trade,' which has brought untold blessings to the working men of the United Kingdom."

One striking feature of the letters in this chapter is the recurring picture of a people angrily watching corn kept back from the market for a rise.   Now that no such thing is possible except to great speculators like Mr. Leiter, this form of social friction is, happily, absent.   Were the bread tax reinstituted the occasion, and with it the hatred, would certainly revive.   Protection is not only the cause of poverty, it is also a force making for social disintegration.

The following letter appeared in the *Daily News* towards the end of January, 1904 :—

"SIR,—I, too, can remember the 'good old times' that Sir Richard Tangye writes about. Wheaten bread was selling at an exorbitant price, and very little came to the share of the working classes.

"Before the potato famine their food largely consisted of that diet ; it was known as 'taters and shake-over,' a little salt being shaken over the potatoes.

"After the disease spread amongst the potatoes, barley meal was greatly used, horse beans and peas occasionally. Swede turnips, with a small piece of bread handed to each round the table, oftentimes constituting the dinner. How could it be otherwise ? Perhaps a labourer, his wife, and several children had to subsist on seven or eight shillings a week.

"No wonder that men were riotous and clamorous ; no wonder that they were shot down in my own native county town in the West of England because they clamoured for bread for their wives and little ones, who were starving.

"The above facts are not what have been read in story books, but what have been seen and felt and known, and this is the state of things that Mr. Joseph Chamberlain, of Birmingham, and his Tariff Commissioners, with well-filled purses, wish to bring us back to.—Yours, &c.,   "G. CHAMBERS.

"Weybridge, *February 3rd.*"

Mr. Alfred Wilkens, of The Avenue, Southampton, sends a short communication, which he calls "Recollections of Protection." Though he writes from that address, his remarks apparently refer to Berkshire :—

"The word Protection reminds me of the miserable undergarments and the long Holland pinafore overall of nearly all boys up to fourteen years of age, but most of all, the 3/- per gallon for the baker's loaf, the usual price being 2/6 per gallon. Brown sugar was 7½d. per pound, and of loaf sugar it was quite a treat to get a lump, for it was 1/- per pound;

tea 6/- per pound. Meat, poultry, butter, and cheese were never tasted more than once or twice a week. Poor people were glad of the tea-leaves from the houses of the rich, and it was thought a great privilege to be the lucky ones to get them. O! the misery of it all! Poor farm labourers in Berkshire, with 8/- or 9/- per week, and large families to keep, had to get up at five o'clock a.m. to fetch the family's water from the village well, some quarter of a mile away or more, as the case might be, with shoes heavy enough to tire them out before they started the day's work. I am almost ashamed to tell you what these poor creatures had to eat. I remember after the repeal of the Corn Laws, when bread was 8d. per gallon and butter 8d. per pound, I have been to the shop with a shilling and brought home half pound of butter and a gallon of bread for 1/-, and I have paid 9d. for a quartern loaf in the old Protection days.

"I remember just before the Crimean War, when bread was at its cheapest, and farmers wanted 28/- a quarter for wheat, and if they had got it they would have wanted 30/- or 32/-. The great trouble with them was, they were never satisfied. The largest consumers began to import wheat, and have continued to do so at a much cheaper price than we can produce it. I think it will be a great shame to put a tax on the poor man's principal food. If the farmers and the masses had not been neglected by the richest country in the world, but had had the advantages of other poorer countries in education, they would not be in the state they are to-day."

From a letter which appeared in the *Daily News* early in February, 1904, we take the following :—

"At a gathering of Mid-Sussex Liberals the following interesting letter was read from a well-known farmer :—

"'I am one of a family of eleven, and six of us are farming at the present time. I well remember when my father was paying 50s. per acre for the land and 10s. per acre tithe. Wheat was then 50s. to 60s. per quarter. About 1856, in July and August, we did not get two dry days for six weeks, and the whole of the hay was only fit for dung.   The wages were very low, the working man only getting 8s. to 11s. per week.

"'Talk about ever tasting butcher's meat! It was out of the question.   Cabbage and bacon all the year round, and sometimes very little of that.   We children did most of the work on the farm, so were indulged with a taste of roast beef about once a month, on a Sunday, on which day we had a cup of tea. Other days we had broth and skim milk. When I read that Mr. Chamberlain's scheme was going to give more employment and more wages, it made me think of the days before we got the greatest blessing this country ever enjoyed—Free Trade.

"'We are asked to believe that a 2s. tax on corn will not raise the price of bread.   I ask what benefit would a two or four shilling per quarter tax on corn benefit a farmer?   I say none at all.   Even a dairy farmer would have to pay much more for grains and everything else which he requires for the farm and his own household.

" 'What farmers want is not Protection, but reduced rents.   The land they are paying 20s. to 30s. per acre for can only keep them slaves all their lives.   A lot of the land in Sussex is not worth more than 5s. per acre for a man to get a fair, honest living.   Paying this last-named rent, he could afford to buy a bit of dung from London and elsewhere.   That is what the average farmer cannot do, because he is compelled to sell what he ought to consume.   What for?   Why, to get the rent and taxes ready.   I have two or three brothers farming now under Lord Boyne ; the land is let according to the value of it—from 5s. per acre to about 15s.   What Sussex farmers want is more Lord Boynes, and then they could live where they now only exist.' "

WESSEX UNDER PROTECTION

CHAPTER IV

WESSEX UNDER PROTECTION

Miss Benjafield writes :—

"In the quaint old town of Stalbridge, in Dorsetshire, which is situated on the borders of Thomas Hardy's Wessex, are still to be found old inhabitants who remember the bad old times of Protection.

"One white-haired old woman whom I was talking to recently told me her tale of those days. Her father and mother, she said, brought up ten children. They all lived in a tiny cottage on a common. In this there was only one bedroom! The father worked on a farm near, earning 7s. a week.

"Barley flour was then 10s. a bushel; tea, 5s. 4d. a lb.; green tea, 8s.; sugar, 6d. or

8d. a lb.   Bacon, however, was 4d. a lb., and butter 8d.   (Of course the rise in the price of butter and bacon is not the result of Free Trade ; but of the facility with which produce can now be transmitted to the large cities and towns, where higher prices can be demanded. With the advance of the locomotive the rise must have come, whether Free Trade or Protection predominated.   Therefore the labourer would have been even more destitute under continued Protection.)   There was not much they could choose from.   The family lived on flatcakes, about an inch thick, made of coarse barley flour, and baked in a little black iron crock with three legs, such as are now imitated in the construction of coal-scuttles, bowls, &c. These crocks, which cost from 8d. to 2s. or 3s., were hung on hooks over the fire, and in them everything that had to be cooked was cooked.

" Treacle they used instead of sugar, as it was cheaper.   Beef and mutton they were unable to purchase ; but on Sundays, perhaps, the father and mother would have a rasher or two of bacon, whilst the children looked on with longing eyes and whispered to each other (for they would not have dared to ask or make a complaint aloud; parents, even in cottages, were sterner in those stern times) that when they 'grew up' they also would have their rasher! But when they were men and women the time produced John Bright, and they fed on richer food than rashers.

"Sometimes an ounce of tea was bought; but it would not always go round enough, and the old woman, then the little Elizabeth, can well recollect that at such a critical moment the inventive genius of her mother, urged on by necessity, showed itself. A little piece of barley-cake was put before the fire till it was baked black; this was then crumbled and added to the scanty tea-pot — result, more tea!—what matter if it was more barley tea than Chinese? The children had some.

"Some mornings the little ones would rise early and go out into the fields to pick Charlie (a field weed) or nettle tops; these were boiled in the 'crock' and eaten to savour the barley-cake.

11

"Children were not compelled to go to school, so that many grew up without the knowledge of reading. Indeed, an elderly grocer told me that at one time the letters of the town were delivered by a post-woman who could not read! He used to take his own, and tell her which were for the next house.

"In the time of the Crimean War the poor were in great distress. The authorities made a subscription, and with it bought sacks of dried peas; these were served out by the pint to the people, and on these they subsisted.

"An old farmer can remember the time when the price of the 4-lb. wheaten loaf was 1s. 6d. And he has seen the men on his father's farm, when they fed the pigs with barley-meal, take a little of the meal aside and, mixing it thicker, eat it to stay their hunger! 'The husks that the swine did eat' they ate truely in the time of Protection, yet Mr. Chamberlain advocates a second Protection period, and promises the working man, as a result, a fat pig! The country must look at facts, not words. In

Stalbridge at that time the number of inhabitants averaged about 2,000. Yet the butcher only 'killed' half a cow a week—the other half going to a neighbouring town. Now, in the time of Free Trade, in spite of all the taxes caused by the war, &c., and though the population is reduced to 1,600 or 1,700, the butchers kill two cows a week, besides sheep and pigs."

From another interesting communication, contributed by the Rev. W. D. Sargeaunt, of Stoke Abbott Rectory, Dorset, we take the following :—

" I am the vicar in a village of 1,300 inhabitants. Twenty years ago, when the village was much smaller, all worked on the land. Now there is a flourishing trade, and the agricultural labourer is a *rara avis*. A field of twenty acres, let out in allotments, forms part of the glebe. I am going to tell the story of one of my tenants, an old man of 73, who farms about four acres of the said field, and brings his rent to me regularly at the end of the half year, Just fifty years ago my hero, then 23 years old, was a married man with one child, a girl not two years old. When the family got up in the morning there was nothing in the house but a crust of bread, and the bread-winner out of work. He started off early to look for work, and walked all day. He was not successful. Let me tell the story of that evening in his own words : ' I came in at night quite done for. I said to my wife, " Have you a bit of victual ? I think I shall die." " There's the bit of crust we left last night in the cupboard," she cried ; " we haven't touched a bit all day." So we got the crust out of the cupboard and crumbled it into a basin and poured some hot water over it, and we sat down opposite one another. My wife and I had a big spoon each, and we gave the child a small spoon and set her between us. But you see, she was too small to get hold of the spoon, so she threw it down and dashed her hand into the hot water again and again, and crammed the bread into her mouth as it might be a wild beast, she was so hungry. Then my wife and I threw down our spoons and sat and cried at one another like babies, and that's all we had that day. The child eat the bread, and my wife and I we drank the water.' Farm wages then were eight shillings a week, and before long the man was working for a butcher who farmed a bit of land. 'My master used to send me in a bit of meat every week, and I let it run on. When it had gone some time, I said to myself, "This won't do, I must pay up." So I said to my master, "Master," I said, "how do we stand?" "Stiffish," he said. "How much do I owe you?" I said. "Between four and five pounds," he said. "Well," said I, "I never owed nothing yet, and what's more, I won't owe you this." So from that time till I had paid off that account, me and mine never eat a bit of meat. We were just going to put in the wheat, and one day I put in ten acres of wheat. I thought I should have fallen on the ground. The time came round for putting in the barley. We put in the wheat in October and the barley in March ; and when we put in the barley I worked a whole day at that and didn't have a bit of meat, and hadn't had since we put in the wheat; so bit by bit I paid off that account.' 'And how came it,' I asked, 'that you had run up so large a bill?' 'Ah! there you are,' he cried. 'He kept sending me in more than I asked for. I said, "Send me about a couple of pounds," and he'd send in four. And there's many as do the same to-day if you let 'em. Ah! but I'm wrong. I did have a bit of meat once. One day my master sent me to the next village to fetch his children back from school—they were put out for their schooling, and I was sent to meet 'em and fetch 'em home. And that night, when I came in, my master gave me a bit of supper, and I had a bit of meat with it.'"

Mr. Sargeaunt's old friend, who managed to pay off a debt of between £4 and £5 out of a wage of 8s. a week, seems to have done very well when, later, wages in Dorset rose to 11s., accompanied as the rise in wages was with the general fall in the price of food. He joined the Co-operative Society, and contrived to save money both in it and in the Savings

Bank, and with his savings was enabled to lease the glebe allotment from Mr. Sargeaunt's predecessor. The old man is still living, or was last February.

Mr. Thomson, Round Hill Lodge, Henstridge, Blandford, Dorset, writes :—

" I have been thinking, as you suggested the other day in *Reynolds's*, that we old men owe a duty to the younger generation, who know nothing about the old Protection days, and that we should let them know what we toilers had to endure during that period.   I can speak from my own experience, having lived the first twenty years of my life when we had Protection, and when it was a hard struggle for the poor to live at all.   I well remember when I and my brothers and sisters had often to go to bed at night without any supper, and be contented by thinking, and sometimes dreaming, that we may be able to get a small bit of barley-cake in the morning for our breakfast. I was born at Stourton Caundle, a small village in North Dorset, in 1826.   My father was an agricultural laborer, and he worked on one farm for more than thirty years, and was considered by his master to be a good work-man, as he could turn his hand to any kind of work that was required to be done on the farm; and his pay was only seven shillings a week, and there were himself, our mother, and six children to live. All kinds of food was then very dear. It was barley-cake and potatoes from day to day, and not enough of that; and, as for bread, we scarcely ever saw any, and meat was far beyond our reach. Moist sugar was 6d. per pound, tea 4d. per ounce; wheaten flour was four shillings per peck of 14 lbs. Bread was sold at from 9d. to 1/- the 4-lb. loaf. Coal was 1/10½ per cwt. Clothing was also very dear. Poor children were often seen running about the streets in rags and barefooted—a pitiable sight to see—and almost starving. There was no day-school in the parish, and not six agricul-tural labourers in the village who could read or write, where the population was about 400. I myself was sent out in the fields to work when only 8 years old, and got only one shilling for

seven days' work, keeping the crows from the
farmer's corn and doing other jobs, and had no
more pay when I was ten years old.   I trust
all working men will be wise in time, and not
be gulled by Joseph or any one else as to
higher wages, &c., if their Protection scheme
is carried out.   They must know already that
he has deceived them two or three times before
by false promises.   So they must now be on
their guard and only vote for Free Traders."

"J. S. B.," late of Axminster, Devon, gives
us a clear little picture of his early life :—

"My mother, more than sixty years ago, was
left a widow with four young children in
Axminster.   In the course of business she was
expected to take from farmers, who were her
customers, corn, which she would have ground
at the town mills, and make her home-made
bread.   I shall never forget a year, about
sixty years ago, when, in consequence of a
wet harvest, the wheat was grown out, and
when made into bread it would stick to our
teeth, or could be stretched out like putty.
Such stuff, since the admission of foreign

wheat, would, of course, be rejected for human food.

" I also remember an old friend, about the same time, telling us he had, on the previous morning, seen a family breaking their fast with swedes fried in fat. I related this 20 years ago at a public meeting in Axminster, when a man in the audience stood up and said, 'That had been his experience many times, and, what is more, we had to steal the swedes to have them or nothing.'"

Next we have a truly tremendous picture of life in the early part of last century. The writer of it is Mr. S. L. Jacob, of North View, Warminster. Perhaps nowhere do we get a more realistic view of the times than in this letter :—

" I perceive you are about to publish a book respecting the bad old times of Protection. I was born in Frankfort Street, Plymouth, in 1826. When I was five years of age I had the typhoid fever. When I recovered the doctor ordered change of air. My parents took me to my uncle's, J. Besley, at Carthstone Farm, in the parish of Milverton, Somersetshire. I was allowed to run wild for a few months. At six years of age I was sent into the fields with the aprentice boys and girls of about the same age, to keep pigs, clean turnips, drive oxen and horses at plough, and various other field work. Sometimes the horses went away with heavy loads of corn and long distances, then we were called up at two or three o'clock to bring back the extra horse that helped the load a few miles over the hills. We had many bitter winters during the nine years I was with my uncle, and I have often been nearly frozen as well as the other poor little mortles. We had to force on our hard, hob-nailed boots (weighing from three to four pounds) over feet swolen with chilblains, and 'kebe heles,' that is, with a hole in them, with running matter. One winter my left foot was frost-bitten.

" The delekit children were soon kiled, in fact one was knocked over the stones by my great-aunt, and her neck broken, and no notice was taken of it. My great-aunt was a very passionate woman. She used to lash us with her riding-whip for the least thing, and when my uncle came in she would not let him rest until he had thrashed us well. We used to have bread and skim milk for breakfast, and skimed milk cheese, like leather. We used to call the bread and milk ' Skie-blue and barley-sinkers.' Sunday mornings we had the cream aded to the milk that we might know the day. Our farm was about five hundred acres. We worked 35 horses and 24 bullocks, the farm being three parts tilege. Our nine men that were indoor hands slept in one room—all they had to cover them was a doules sheet and a coloured counterpain. In winter they put any amount of sacks under the quilt. They were not allowed any light to dress or undress. They had a rushlight to attend to the cattle. They had to strike a light with flint and steel.

"We had breakfast at 7, and whatever the weather was, we did not return to have any dinner until we had ploughed our acer, that was the day's work. Then we had to fry our bacon, rusty as a horseshoe, and potatoes, or whatever we could get, for ourselves. Our bread was mildued one half the time, for we baked only once in three weeks in summer, and every five weeks in winter. Then we boys had to scrape away the snow with our hands to pull the turnips, and wash them at the trough out of doors, as well as the potatoes, when the water would freaze; then peal the potatoes in an open shed, and grate them to make starch. We used to do all the scouring with a 'wod' of wet straw diped in wood-ashes—no polishing-paste then. If we had anything rusty to polish, such as bits and stirips, we put them in the tub where the new cider was made, for a few hours, then you could wipe off all the rust with your fingers and thumb. If at any time we wanted to black our boots, we weted the brush, and rubed it over the side of the great boiler the pork was boiled in, so the fat and sute did for blacking.

"Our indoor men received from 2/- to 2/6 per week. They wore a 'doulis' shirt, bare breast, winter and summer. If they had a waistcoat it was generally made of lambskin or moleskin. They used to preserve the skins of moles. They caught a lot of them. Some of them wore long smock frocks, others any old coat they could pick up, cord trousers or briches, with yarn stockings, boots that weiyed from 6 to 7 lbs., which they washed and greased once a week in order to go to church. Very seldom any of them had any other clothing to ware to church, where they where bound to attend or stand the consequence. The farm-hands had to sit in an end galerey in church, and the man that had charge of them was armed with a long goard, such as we used to drive the bullocks at plough, and every now and then you would here the sound throughout the church of the strokes of the rod on some of their backs; and if they rebeled they were put in the stocks just outside the church door for every one to gear at as they left the church.

"Almost every six months we had a tailor come to repair the clothes and make for the household.   He would sit on an old table and stick from morning till night for 6d. per day, and food and logins.   The sadler would come also for the same pay.   There was no time for piano-playing in those days.   The women had to milk the cows, feed the pigs, poultry, calves, and healp in the fields.   They used to commence washing every Monday at 2 a.m. My great-aunt would get up and work with them all the day till late at night, and row them all the time.   There was no soap powder or anything to make the work easey in those days, no coper, all the water had to be made boil over a wood fire on the harth.   We never had a bit of coles in the house the nine years I was there.   We had to go about one mile to post a letter.   The letter was placed in a split goard with the money for postage—1/- if for Plymouth.   The mail-coach passed Watenew, a village between Wiveliscome and Bampton.   We handed the goard to the gard while the horses galloped on.   If we expected a letter we had to go to Wiveliscome to fetch it, full three miles.

"As for morality, there was just as much as with the dogs and cats, which reminds me of what my mother used to say, 'Where is a lot of men and women servants living together, they are alway scratching or kissing.'

"I have given you a breefe sketch of indoors, I will now give you a slight sketch of out. There being a large amount of tilleg on our farm, and all the work had to be done by hand, even the thrashing the corn. We had about 30 men at work that lived out of the house. They worked from daylight until dark in the winter, and from 6 a.m. until any time the master wanted them in the summer without any extra pay. In harvest time they often worked 18 hours, but then they had supper, for which we provided by killing any animal that was unsaleable, such as an old boar or ram, or a bullock to save its life, to keep it from dieing. Twenty-eight of these men had 6/- per week and a quart of cider, one of them had 7/-, and the headman 8/-. Only two or three of them could read or write. How could they learn? They had to go to work before they where able to walk over a ploud field without falling over the bigest clods. The National school was 5 miles from our farm, that was Milverton ; and if it had been nearer the parents could not afford to send them. If the children did not learn at an early age, how was the family to be kept on 6/- a week? Our labourers brought their breakfasts with them, which consisted, as a rule, of a piece of corse bread—you would call it black—and a bunch of garlic or some onions. Their wives (I might well call them their slaves), or their children (in fact, they were all slaves, and mostly brutes as well) brought their dinners, which generally consisted of mashed potatoes and turnips, with a scrap of ' must ' to moisten it. What they call 'must' is lard, and many times they could not get the must. Fortunately there was no potato disease. Then they were perfect ; the crops were enormous, and they were sold in Plymouth, the 'lords' at 1/6 per bag, 140 lbs., the 'ladys' at 1/3. If the potatoes had been as dear and as wastful as now, the familys must have starved with the flour at £4 4s. per sack. The turnips they drew principally from our fields. The wheate they bought was tailings, with all the seeds and grit in it; that they took to the mill and had it ground fine, so as to use the whole of it in their bread. No wonder it was black, and in bad harvests it was milekey, so that you could eat with a spoon.

"We had several bad harvests in the thirties. One in particular. It rained every day, more or less, for six weeks during harvest time. We had 375 acres in corn that year. We saved one field of wheat, 4 acres, which was very earley. All the rest of the corn grew out, so that was impossible to make bread of it; so we bought some French barley, and that, when made into bread, was so gritte we did not know how to eat it. The distress that year was fearful. What our labourers had for supper was a conglomeration of vegetables stued. You may well suppose they stole whatever they could lay their hands on, and no wonder!

"I don't think there was a month whilst I

was on the farm but one or more of our men was in Taunton lock-up ; and can you wonder at it? They were like hungery wolves. Continually we had sheep stolen. One December we had 21 fat turkeys stolen that we had been feeding for Tiverton Xmas market. Fowels we had to put under lock and key. A coper they used to boil barley in for the horses was taken out to be repaired. Before it could be put in again it was stolen. As for clothing, it was scarcely enough for desensey. The poor women! Can you believe it? I have known them confined one day, wash their clothes the next, the third day put the baby in an old box or basket, and take it with them into the fields to wead corn or pick stones, for which they received 6d. per day, and glad to get it to put a garment on their backs.

"G. Nation had a wife and 7 children, all sons. They had a stone-floored kitchen, and one small bedroom. After struggling on in misery, some friends helped them to emegrate and they all did well.

"J. Street, a wife and 7 daughters, all

sleeping in one small bedroom. This man was duble as well off as most of the others; for he had 1s. per day pension. He was in the battle of Waterloo.

"James Stone, a wife and 5 children, living and sleeping in one room over a cow-shed, on a bed of straw.

"J. Roseter, wife and 3 children, sleeping in a downstair room, with a stone floor, a guttar of water running through the room. He had charge of our ferets and rat terriers. They were in the same room. He had a few fowels which roosted in the same. These he had stolen from some one, but was not trased.

"J. Sayer and his wife lived over a tuckin mill. He was just married and lived with his father and mother and two grown-up daughters in two rooms. The daughters were prostitutes.

"G. Jewel had a bed-riden wife. They lived and slept in one room. He was better off than many, for he was a marine and had a pension of 10d. per day. He should have had 1s., but he had the small bone of his arm broken in boarding a French ship in the battle of Trefalger. He was sent below to the doctor, who wanted to take his arm off, because he had £1 1s. for every limb he took off. George said, 'You shall not take my arm off!' The doctor said, 'You dog, you shall not have a "smart!"' That was 1s. a day, so he only had 10d., and the bone was never set; but he was able to work as well as any man.

" J. Sayer was a very clever man. He went to Australia in '48 with my help, and made enough at the digins to retier.

" You will suppose my uncle made his fortune owing to paying such low wages. Nothing of the kind. My uncle failed, as nearly half the farmers in the county at that time, owing to the high rent and bad harvests. His wife and only daughter died early and left him depen-dent upon relatives. If he had not taken that farm he had capital sufficient to keep himself and family in comfort. His three sons went to Australia and are weathy men.

" When I was 15 I left my uncle, and my relations put me an apprentice to a miller for three years, and paid him an ansum yearly premium. This miller went to that mill in 1836 with 7s. 6d. in cash, and an old spavin horse. He left about 12 years after with thousands, although he rarely came from market sober. He told me himself that all the flour he sent to Yap, a flour merchant at Plymouth, he had £1 1s. a sack profit; and Yap sold to the bakers at 3s. per sack profit, but the poor had to pay for it.

" The reason he got such profit was, Lindon the corn merchant would say, 'Here, John, there will be more duty on the corn on such a date; you take this cargo of wheat and pay when you can.' I use to say to him, ' But what about the poor starving women and children?' He would say, ' They can live on fish and potatoes.' I have said the potatoes were plentiful and cheap then, when there was no disease; and you could buy more fish in Plymouth then for 2d. than now for 1s., when there was no rail to take it away. If the wretches are able to put the duty on corn now what will be the consequence?

Our farmers with the rent they have to pay cannot grow corn for less than 50s. per quarter. Nothing less than 12s. per quarter will do. You may think the miller named above would be generous to those he employed. Not a bit of it. When I went with him at 15, he discharged a man and I took his place, and I and another apprentice ran the mill day and night for months together. That will show if men give better wages when they are making large profits. From there I went to St. Austell, in Cornwall; there I was when the bread riots brok out. After the destruction of a lot of property the soldiers arrived. Then they took 17 of the ringleaders and sent them to Bodmin, only for trying to get bread."

The following letter illustrates the keen interest taken by the old people who have known Protection in the controversy. The writer, Mr. John Gill, of Penrhyn, Cornwall, is almost the oldest of all our correspondents.

"I had read to me from the *New Age* that you invite those who have passed through the old days of Protection to write to you on the subject. I am well qualified to do so, being over 92 years of age, and I have a keen memory of passing events from childhood to the present time. I recollect events that transpired when very young, including the tolling of the church bell at the death of Princess Charlotte in 1817, before the late Queen's parents were married.

" The present generation can have no conception of the state and condition of the labouring people when Protection was rampant. Every article that could be named for the use of man being taxed, their food, their clothing, their furniture, their mode of travelling, and many other habits and customs were totally different to those of the present time. The wages of agricultural labourers were from 1s. to 1s. 6d. per day, of trades from 2s. to 2s. 6d. per day. Their food consisted principally of barley bread ; and, in Cornwall, of potatoes and pilchards, and they had barely sufficient of these. The clothing was of the coarsest kind, consisting of swan-skin, corduroy and fustian—the latter on Sundays. Broadcloth was rarely to be seen on a working man's back. A letter from London cost a shilling, taking three days to bring it. Women servants wore bed-gowns of the most ugly kind. This state of things did not apply to the rich and well-to-do, who could then ride in their carriages, and fare sumptuously, as they can now. It was the labouring classes who suffered by Protection, and it will bring certain ruin to them if they are so ignorant and foolish in their own interests to allow it to be introduced again. I well remember the years of 1829–1832, when the country was in a ferment, and on the verge of a civil war on the question of Catholic Emancipation, and on the Reform Bill before it passed in 1832. Then followed the great agitation on the Corn Laws, in which Villiers, Cobden and Bright were three of the most prominent pleaders, in which I took a great interest. In the years 1840–1 I was appointed to the office of overseer in this town. For these years it was a painful task to go from street to street seeking rates, where the inhabitants had neither work, money, nor bread, when the Corn Laws were in full force, and the agitation against them had become very keen. Sir Robert Peel's Government was formed to protect them; but the Irish famine intervened and broke them down. The trade of the country then began to improve in all directions, and it would have done so much faster had it not been for the guilty promoters of the Crimean War, which was a curse to the country.

" I cannot see to read, and I only know of present passing events by getting them read to me. I have written this letter by feeling my way, and I can just dimly see to read what I have written."

The following is an extract from a letter contributed to the *Westminster Gazette* of June 8, 1903, by Mr. Richard Robbins, of Upper Holloway. As will be seen, it also relates to Cornwall :—

" At the date of my birth—August 3, 1817— the Protectionist system was at its height; and it was felt most keenly by the workers because of the way in which it kept up the price of bread. Parliament had just forbidden the importation of all foreign wheat, when the price was below 80/- a quarter ; and the labourers in my part of the country could scarcely have a wheaten loaf from one year's end to the other, having to put up with barley bread.

"My home was the ancient borough of Launceston, in Cornwall, which at that time was an Assize town as well as a marketing centre for a large agricultural district, and the home of an old-established woollen industry. It was, therefore, a favourable specimen of a country place, and yet when William Cobbett visited it at the time I was four years old— and my recollections begin in that year, 1821, when George IV. was crowned, for I was present at the local rejoicings—he was told by a tradesman (and the statement is to be found in his "Rural Rides") that the people in general there could not even afford to have a fire in ordinary, and that he himself had paid threepence for boiling a leg of mutton at another man's fire!

"But if food and fuel were dear for a trades-man, how much dearer did they seem to the labourer and the artizan! We are being told that if Protection is brought back to us wages will rise and the working man be better off. What was the case in my young days? I will tell the working men of to-day, and let them judge for themselves, pledging myself not to make a single statement I cannot vouch for as having seen for myself the facts.

"The wages of shoemakers at the time of which I am speaking were from 9/6 to 10/6 a week; and their hours of work were from six o'clock in the morning to eight at night from Lady Day to the first Monday after the 8th of September, and from eight in the morning to eight at night the rest of the year, with half an hour allowed for breakfast in the summer, an hour for dinner, and half an hour for tea—about twelve hours' daily work for an average of 10/- a week, and bread at the price it then was. They were given one whole holiday in the year, and that was Christmas Day, for they had to work all Good Friday;

but they had half a day off on Easter Monday, Whit Monday and Tuesday, and Mayor-choosing day, and the evening off on St. Crispin's Day. I myself knew a good workman at the leading boot-shop in the town whose average wage was never over 9/- weekly throughout his life, not even when bread was 2/- the quartern loaf.

"Carpenters and masons were paid a little better, their wages ranging from 11/- to 12/- a week, and their hours of work being from six in the morning to six in the evening for eight months in the year, and from seven to five the other four months. The wages of tailors were from 10/- to 12/-; and they worked from six a.m. to eight p.m., except in November, December, January, and February, when the hours were from eight to eight; and they were allowed an hour for dinner, but if they wanted tea it had to be brought to them as they sat on their shop boards. Woolstaplers and fell-mongers worked from six to six for from 9/- to 10/6 per week, while day labourers were paid from 7/6 to 8/6 in the town, and 7/- to 8/- in the country, the wages coming partly in the latter case out of the poor rate! The custom when I was a boy was for able-bodied men to attend a vestry or parish meeting, and their services to be put up to the biggest bidder among the farmers present. Sometimes the price bid was no more than 10d. a day, and this would be made up to 1/2 or 1/3 by the parish. What was the result? The men, who would have been free and independent under a better system, were compelled to be paupers.

"I do not say that there were no working men who were better paid than those I have mentioned. The curriers and hatters, for instance, were the aristocrats among the arti-sans of the town; but they were the excep-tions, and, though they earned good money, the ropers and the woolstaplers and the basket makers had no more than from 8/- to 9/- a week."

We close with a short letter from the other side of the Bristol Channel. Mr. E. Green, Rose Cottage, Brits Neuton, near Tewksbury, writes :—

" I see in the *Methodist Times* that you would like to hear somethink about the miseries of Protection.   I'm sending you a few lines as I know to be true.   I seen Lord Rosbery's letter in the paper.   That started me writing.   I sent the like of this to 4 different papers.   Seventy-two years ago, when I went to school at Upton-on-Severn, I knew several children who did not go home to dinner because they could not have any ; and when I began housekeeping, that was over fifty years ago, then bread was 5 lbs. for 1/-, and 2½ lb. for 6d., sometimes dearer than that, brown sugar 5d. per lb., and lump from 6d. to 8d. per lb., tea 4/- per lb., not so good as we get now for 1/6, salt 6d. per lb., and I knew farm labourers having 6s. a week, and ten being the highest.   Clothes were dear. Working people could have nothing better than prints for the women, men codorroy and smock-frocks.   As for meat, working people did not get a bit once a month.   I'm a shoe-maker.   When I worked journeyman in Protection times, I only had 2/9 for making a pair

of men's boots. I work for myself now. If I
employ any one I have to give them 4/9. We
believe in Free Trade. We don't want any
Protection."

A striking feature of these Wessex letters is
their grim realism. Probably the district
suffered as severely as any, and far more than
some ; but that hardly accounts for the specially
graphic character of the writing. West Country
people must have long memories, and may, we
may safely say, be trusted to remain staunch
Free Traders till long after the last "protected"
generation has passed away.

PROTECTION IN THE NORTH OF
ENGLAND

CHAPTER V

PROTECTION IN THE NORTH OF ENGLAND

How people fared in the county of Yorkshire the following interesting and pathetic letter will show. The immense power which the helplessness of the people placed in the hands of their employers is well illustrated in the writer's account of his treatment as a child. He is Mr. George Oldfield, St. Peter's Street, Norton Malton :—

"My father's native place was Honley, about 7 miles from Huddersfield. His parents were poor working people—so much so that they had to get rid of their children as best they could ; so my father was a town's aprentice to a farmer—he got his food but no wages at a village, Crosland Hill, his master finding him what clothing he thought useful, while he was of age.   After his aprenticeship he went to work in the stone quarreys.   In due time he got maryed, and there was a family of 3 children.   I was the second, and had 2 sisters.   Poor mother died when I was between 2 and 3.   My eldest sister went to work in the factory very early.   I soon had to follow, I think about 9 years of age. What with hunger and hard usage I bitterly got it burned into me—I believe it will stay while life shall last.   We had to be up at 5 in the morning to get to factory, ready to begin work at 6, then work while 8, when we stopped ½ an hour for breakfast, then work to 12 noon; for dinner we had 1 hour, then work while 4.   We then had ½ an hour for tee, and tee if anything was left, then commenced work again on to 8.30.   If any time during the day had been lost, we had to work while 9 o'clock, and so on every night till it was all made up.   Then we went to what was called home.   Many times I have been asleep when I had taken my last spoonful of porige—not even washed, we were so overworked and underfed. I used to curs the road we walked on. I was so weekley and feeble I used to think it was the road would not let me go along with the others. We had not always the kindest of masters. I remember my master's strap, 5 or 6 feet long, about $\frac{3}{4}$ in. broad, and $\frac{1}{4}$ in. thick. He kept it hung on the ginney at his right hand, so we could not see when he took hould of it. But we could not mistake its lessons; for he got hould of it nearly in the middle, and it would be a rare thing if we did not get 2 cuts at one stroke. I have reason to believe on one occasion he was somewhat moved to compassion, for the end of his strap striped the skin of my neck about 3 in. long. When he saw the blood and cut, he actually stoped the machine, came and tied a handkerchief round my neck to cover it up. I have been fell'd to the floor many times by the ruler on the top of the carding, about 8 or 9 feet long, iron hoop at each end. This was done as a change for the strap. For a time I could not tell whether living or dead. At the Coronation of our late beloved Queen Victoria I was a scoller at the Buxton Road Wesleyan Sunday School, Huddersfield, before the present Wesleyan Chapel was built. So the Coronation day was fixed. I had neither shoes nor clogs to go in, but, like others, I was not to be bet that way, so I asked another lad, much biger than myself, to lend me his clogs for the day. He did lend them to me. They were verey much to big, quit down at the heels, and up at the frunt. I was not to be stoped by trifles, so I went to the grand affair—to me anyhow. I marched in the procession to the old market square at Huddersfield, and afterwards enjoyed a splendid tee. Shurely this was one of the brightest days of my life ! About this time, or soon afterwards, that Heaven-sent messenger, Lord Shaftesbury, got a Bill passed to shorten the hours in the factory. I read of his Lordship's houlding a meeting in Leeds, where some 200 children or more were at the meeting, and not one of them but was a cripple, as also where both my sister and myself were crippled for life. I do not know I ever had a new suit of cloths—I may have had odd things new. My clothing generally was made out of old clothes. I remember right well my trouses being so bad that I had to perform some operation on them, and as Sunday was the onley day at liberty, I sat in bed that day, and completed the work by cutting the whole backside out, and fixing fresh pieces of cloth in to cover my back with. I am not fond of Sunday work. I wish nothing worse were don on this God-given day. So we children worked 12½ hours a day for 8d. or 4/- per week. If flower was not more than 3/6 per stone we thought it cheap; but it was often 4/-, 5/- and 5/6 per stone, and other things dear in proportion. It was about 1842. Things were simply appaling. There was disquiet in Lancashire, bread rioting, and hundreds of people came down the 2 dales leading to Huddersfield, stoping mills from working by drawing the shuttles, letting off the water supply, knocking out steam plugs to put out the fires. Both men, youths, and girls, with handkerchief on their head, came into the market place at Huddersfield. The cavelery were called out. Some feind of a brute called a magistrait, after making the cavelery drunk, and gave the order to put the hungrey people between the devil and the deep sea—a work that required feinds to do, to their eternal shame. When corn was 80/- per quarter, farmers kept it back to keep the price up, and went about as huxtors trying to sell to privat individuals, and the blood-succers, their landlords, took it out of them.

"So as the Factory Act came in force we did not work so late at nights. I joined the evening mechanics' class at Huddersfield to improve myself a little. My father got to be foreman at the quarry, but he did not know a letter or a figure. He had a good memory, and after hearing an order read, he could work it out. I should question if he got 6d. per week more for being foreman. I used to keep his books, learnt him his letters, and to read and make out his orders. After a time be sent me to a free school at Seed Hill, Huddersfield, to get polished in my schooling. Since then I have seen a good deal of the world. I have circled the globe, and rought with people of many nations, but never witnessed anything so wicked and degrading as the old degrading, dear-food times. The dearer it is the worse it is. May God prevent a return to such wickedness, and in His great mercy spare the nation such a trial. It shall be my daily prayer."

Mr. A. S. Ashton, of Belmont Park, Leeds, gives several interesting facts about the state of trade in Lancashire and elsewhere in 1841. He says: "There were 2,000 houses empty in Preston in 1841, and in spite of the Corn Laws the farmers were badly off; the labourers were poor— so poor that they were driven to desperation, so that there were in one and a half years 300 to 400 incendiary fires, destroying corn and hay ricks. In Leeds, in 1841, there were

20,000 persons whose average earnings were under 1/- a week. In Birmingham, one-fifth of the population were in receipt of parochial relief. In Birmingham many of the masters were near ruin. The state of Paisley was a source of alarm to Sir Robert Peel. In Manchester 12,000 families, after having pawned every article of furniture and of dress with which they could possibly dispense, were supported by voluntary contributions. In the winter of 1842 the state of things in Bolton was terrible. As many as 1,500 houses in the borough were unoccupied. The earnings of 1,000 families averaged only 1/2 per head per week; more than half the beds in their possession were filled with straw, and they had among them 466 blankets—not quite one to every ten persons—whilst only one-half could boast the humble luxury of a change of linen."

Mr. William Glazier, St. Edmond's, Worsley Road, Hampstead, sends an excellent article, from which we make the following lengthy extract Mr. Glazier's long experience, to-

gether with the unique position he occupied
for securing information, make his testimony
valuable. We infer that it mainly deals with
Lancashire conditions, from which county Mr.
Glazier only recently came to London :—

"Born in 1825, the son of a provincial
public baker and flour dealer, my recollections
of industrial life, and of how working men
lived, dates back to the year 1835, when on
the death of my father I had to assist in my
widowed mother's business. To the best of
my recollection, at that period, there was not
much complaining in our streets. In 1836
there was an abundant harvest in this country,
with consequent low prices for bread stuffs. It
was in subsequent years that the pinch began,
when the year of plenty was eaten up by years
of scarcity. In the years 1840 and 1841,
there was a succession of bad harvests, with
the inevitable result that food was not only
dear, but to a very large extent of a very
indifferent quality — such that the meanest
pauper in our land to-day would positively
refuse to eat. As my mother kept a public

bakery, I can testify from my own knowledge that numbers of people at that period largely subsisted upon bread made from rye, and barley meal. In a vast number of cases, even that miserable diet was not forthcoming, potatoes taking its place. The suffering amongst the wages class was intense. Pauperism throughout the country was constantly and steadily on the increase. Not only that, but every kind of crime increased at the same rate. Arson or rick-burning, sheep-stealing or slaughtering, &c., by men rendered desperate or despairing through hunger and want, although sternly punished by a shameful and miserable death on the scaffold, prevailed to an extent of which men in these days have not the slightest conception. But it was not only that pauperism increased, and crime increased, but mortality also increased. Strong men and women were stricken down by it, and the aged and little children were its constant and numerous victims. These were some of the results of that cruel law which sternly forbade the free importation of corn into this country fromabroad, until our own prices had risen to 80/- per quarter. Not only was bread, the common food of the people, taxed, but there was hundreds of articles on which, by the law of England, taxes were levied when goods came into London, or Hull, or Liverpool, or Glasgow, or any other ports of the kingdom. Everything was taxed, and of course the retail price of everything which we had to obtain from abroad was increased in a corresponding if not an increased ratio. Indeed, I think that in all cases, the retail prices of imported articles of general consumption increase in a greater ratio than the amount of the tax itself. I may be wrong, but it has always appeared to me that when the prices of foreign commodities are artificially raised by means of a tax, on coming into this country, the dealers in such commodities must, as a pure matter of legitimate business, charge the consumer with something above and beyond the amount of the tax itself. If he does not do that, his one alternative is to supply his customer with goods of a lower grade or quality. Thus in either case the ultimate consumer, according to my view, has to pay not only the tax, but a more or less amount beyond that. As my purpose, however, is to relate facts rather than express opinions, I will quote some of the prices which we had to pay for articles of everyday use. I will confine myself to quoting some of the prices paid for articles of general consumption. The average price of flour was 3/- and 3/6 per stone of 14 lbs. Tea 6/- per lb., and in many cases 6d. per ounce was charged. Sugar 7d. per lb., and very coarse at that. Raisins 7d. per lb., currants 9d., soap 6d., and so on in like proportion, upon the multitude of articles for everyday use. Contrast these prices with those that are paid to-day. It is perfectly true that some food stuffs are dearer under Free Trade than under Protection. Thus, I can remember butter being from sixpence to tenpence per lb., according to the season. Shoulders of mutton, fivepence halfpenny and sixpence per lb. Now we have to pay not less than one shilling and one and twopence per lb. for butter, and eightpence or ninepence per lb. for mutton ; and a few other articles in similar proportion. But making allowance for such exceptional cases, it is safe to say that the cost price of all kinds of food stuffs averaged fully 25 per cent. more in those days than at the present time. Moreover, my memory carries me back to the days when the vast number of foreign-grown or foreign-produced commodities which are now regarded as almost indispensable necessaries and comforts of life, were not even dreamt of by the commonalty. Tinned foods — ox-tongues from Argentina, salmon from British Columbia, luscious fruits, apricots, peaches, plums, pears, &c., from sunny California, pine-apples at a penny a slice, and bananas from the West Indies, and countless other articles, are all within the reach of a large majority of the British working community. These, and the cheapening of the less luxurious necessaries—good wheaten flour at less than ½d. per lb., sugar 2d., tea 1/6 and 2/-, &c., &c., all indicate a vast change in the condition of the class with which I have been associated all my life—a change brought about without any violence, without wronging anybody. There is not a human being in England who has a loaf less, or a pound of sugar less, or any of these things less, by what was done in 1846 and 1849. There was no violence, no insurrection, no bloodshed, no disorder in bringing about this great improvement in the condition of the wages class. It has been done merely by Parliament becoming more intelligent, and statesmen more intelligent, and by merely tearing up two or three foolish Acts of Parliament, and allowing people their natural freedom to buy and sell where they could buy and sell to the greatest advantage.

"But there is still another change which we have to consider. I allude to the enormous difference in the wages rate received by the industrial classes under the old dispensation and the new. On this point I think that I can also fairly claim to speak with authority. In the year 1839 I was placed as an indoor apprentice to the building trade, and happening to be a somewhat better writer than my master, I came in for a pretty fair share of book-keeping, making out wages lists, and similar clerical work. Thus I was not long in becoming well-acquainted with the wages paid, not only to the men in my own trade, but also to the various sections of handicraftsmen throughout the country, outside the Metropolis. Up to, and for some time after the repeal of the Corn Laws in 1846, the standard rate of wages for carpenters, joiners, cabinet-makers, masons, bricklayers, plasterers, plumbers, painters, wheelwrights, coopers, blacksmiths, &c., was eighteen shillings per week of sixty-four hours. (There was no Saturday half-holiday in those 'good' (?) old times!) Now at three shillings per day, this works out at a fraction under 3¾d. per hour. Think of stalwart men, after serving five, six, or seven years to learn a trade, paying, in a vast number of cases, a substantial premium in addition (my apprenticeship premium was £30), and after all, as skilled workmen, receiving the magnificent wage of threepence three-farthings per hour! As for the unskilled workers, their wages averaged ten shillings per week for agricultural labourers, and from twelve to fifteen shillings for those engaged in other occupations.

" Such, according to my experience, was the rate of wages received by the skilled artisans and labourers of this country, in the years immediately preceding the abolition of the Corn Laws in 1846. Contrast the remuneration which such men receive in 1904. Broadly speaking, wages are certainly double, and in a vast number of cases more than double what they were in my younger days. Thus masons, bricklayers, plasterers, &c., receive from nine to tenpence, and tenpence half-penny per hour. Joiners, whose wages vary in different parts of the country, receive never less than sevenpence, sevenpence halfpenny and up to tenpence per hour. Whilst as to unskilled labour, although wages have prob-ably not advanced in the same proportion all round, they may still be assessed at five or sixpence per hour. Only the other day I saw in the *Manchester City News* that the excavators, or ' navvy's,' employed in Derbyshire were being paid fivepence halfpenny per hour, a wage which, in the old Protectionist days, sixty years ago, was utterly beyond the imaginings of the most skilled artisans of that period.

" These, then, are some of the changes, and marvellous changes they are, which have taken place in the social condition of the millions of workers in this land of ours during the genera- tion with which I have been associated for so many years, and I venture to say that there can scarcely be anything more worth a work- ing man's while at the present time, than examining and endeavouring to clearly com- prehend the cause or causes which has led to that vast increase in the comforts, the conveni- ences, and even the luxuries of life which we now enjoy, and which has made life more worth living than was the case under the Protectionist dispensation.   For myself, I have a firm, an enduring belief that beyond all and everything else, these beneficent changes in the condition of the manual workers of Great

Britain have been chiefly or mainly the result of, first and foremost, AN UNTAXED LOAF, and secondly, the establishment of free and open markets (except when required for revenue purposes) for the purchase of such imported commodities as are essential to the carrying on of our various industries. Hence I am a pronounced Free Trader, a thorough-going opponent of what I honestly believe to be the more than non-moral, the absolutely *im*moral fiscal policy which is being so strenuously engineered by our aggressive and loudly assertive countryman, the ex-Colonial Secretary. It is an immoral policy because it substitutes ' Do unto others as *they do unto you*,' for the Golden Rule, ' Do unto others *as ye would* they SHOULD do unto you.' The former policy embodies the spirit of irritation and revenge. The latter breathes of conciliation and good-will to all men. Mr. Chamberlain declared at Birmingham in May last that one of the two objects of his life has been ' the elevation of the masses of the people, the improvement especially of the condition of the very poor.' A very worthy object truly, one to which I, who during a more than ordinary lengthy life, have been more or less associated with the 'masses of the people,' knowing something of their sorrows, trials, difficulties and temptations, do most fervently wish a God-speed. But I utterly deny that this fiscal policy of the ex-Colonial Secretary will have any such effect.

"For myself, I do not for one moment believe that the British workmen of to-day are desirous of a return to the worn-out fiscal policy of other days. They do not require any shuffling of the cards with regard to their daily bread. They have no faith in politicians of the juggling, thimble-rigging type. 'HANDS OFF THE WORKMAN'S LOAF' is the burden of their cry. Nor do they clamour for a ten per cent. tax upon foreign manufactures. Some of us have a lively recollection of a notable states-man who, some seven or eight years ago, took occasion to ridicule the mildly pessimistic utterances of a political opponent, by publicly declaring, 'I do not sympathise with the great statesman who keeps awake in the silent watches of the night, in constant fear with a perpetual nightmare before him, lest German competition should overpower us. I am convinced that, in spite of all defects, we have power enough to hold the property which has come to us from our ancestors, and that we still have the ability to keep the trades that we have made and to hold them against all competitors.' Further on this gentleman went on to say, ' I believe firmly in National Education, but I believe more in National character, and as long as the English people maintain the qualities of the Anglo-Saxon race, so long I, for one, shall not sympathise with those who are constantly predicting evil.' Brave words truly. Yet who would imagine that he who uttered them was and is the same individual who is now engaged in franticly belittling his country and his country's industrial productions, proclaiming to the world that ' all is not well with British trade. . . . Our exports, the exports of our manufactures, the things that employ most labour to foreign countries—to countries that have tariffs, have been declining and are still declining.'

"Well, if that is the case, where is the 'power' and the 'ability' to keep the trades that we have made against all competitors which we had eight years ago? Is that 'power' and 'ability' of ours gone? If it is, then not all the legerdemain of Mr. Chamberlain and those who have been cozened by the glamour of his words to support him, can avail us to escape the fate of being beaten or worsted in the struggle for existence in the markets of the world. No skulking behind fiscal barriers, as these precious tariff reformers are endeavouring to persuade us, will enable the British workman to hold his own against all competitors. *The nation or community that can produce manufactured commodities the best, cheapest, and most in accordance with customers' wishes and requirements, will assuredly win in the long run.* Those who are purchasers of manufactured commodities, naturally seek to get the most and the best for their money. If our goods are dearer, or inferior to those of our competitors, there is no ground compatiable with the sanity of the buyers, which can be alleged, why they should not prefer the latter. Now unless I am labouring under a very grave misapprehension, it is precisely here where our difficulty comes in. Here is one of the reasons why our trade is falling off to foreign countries, as alleged by Mr. Chamberlain. Our goods are either dearer, or inferior, or not according to customers' requirements. There is no mystery about it. Will the new—no, not new, but old, very old—programme, furbished up by our exceedingly forceful ex-Colonial Secretary, avail for our salvation? Will looking backwards beyond the years 1846 and 1849 give us a ray of hope?

"No! a thousand times No! It is none of these things that will enable us to maintain our footing in the markets of the world. There is only one reason why our goods should be preferred to those of our rivals: *customers must find them equally as good or better at the price.* To this end we must use not only more knowledge, industry, and skill, but above all and beyond everything else we must exercise more conscientiousness in our industrial and commercial life, being resolved at the same time that under no pretence, however speciously maintained, will we assent to a reversal of that policy of free imports, both of food and other commercial products, which has contributed so materially to the happiness, the greatness, and commanding position of this country amongst the nations of the earth."

A return of costs in building the house No. 1, Rye Hill, Newcastle-on-Tyne, in the year 1828, has been sent to us by Mr. Frederick Shaw, of Forest Hall, Northumberland. From it we gather that masons then received 3s. 8d. per day, and their labourers 2s. 2d. This would no doubt be for a ten-hour day, and shows that Mr. Glazier's figures were true for Newcastle as well as for Lancashire. We include here a very striking comparison between the prices of groceries in 1820 and 1903. Mr. L. H. Longman, of Bruton, lately published a leaflet comparing the prices charged by his predecessor in the

same business in the former year and those
actually then obtained by himself. Here is
the comparison :—

UNDER PROTECTION, 1820.				UNDER FREE TRADE, 1903.			
lbs.	£	s.	d.	lbs.	£	s.	d.
2 Lump @ 1/- ...	0	2	0	2 Lump ...	0	0	5
2 Moist @ 9d. ...	0	2	3	3 Moist ...	0	0	6
½ Tea @ 8/- ...	0	4	0	½ Tea @ 1/8	0	0	10
1 Yellow Soap ...	0	0	10	1 Yellow Soap	0	0	3
1 Currants ...	0	1	1	1 Currants ...	0	0	4
1 Raisins	0	0	10	1 Raisins ...	0	0	5
14 Salt	0	4	9	14 Salt	0	0	4
3 Candles @ 9d.	0	2	3	3 Candles ...	0	1	1½
½ Grd. Coffee ...	0	1	8	½ Coffee @ 1/6	0	0	9
1 Starch	0	0	11	1 Starch ...	0	0	4
¼ Pepper	0	1	0	¼ Pepper ...	0	0	5
	£1	1	7		£0	5	8½

An interesting pamphlet, published by
Messrs. Sherratt & Hughes, gives a graphic
idea of affairs in Lancashire on the days of
Protection.   Issued last year (1903) and called
" Protection's 'Good Old Days,'" it consists
of extracts from the life of John Mills. It
describes how, in 1840, crowds of angry men
wandered about drawing out boiler plugs and

thus stopping factories. "Starving and miserable," we read, "they went about in gangs,
forcing their way into houses by terrifying the
inmates ; and emptying pantry and larder, but
I never heard of the poor fellows harming or
insulting child or woman."

"Our brave little mother," the writer goes
on, "had no fears. In the morning, when the
men-folk had left for the foundry, the doors and
windows were kept fast, we sometimes acting
as scouts. So it came about that one day,
running home, we cried, 'They are coming !—
lots of them !' Immediately all went in, and
the doors were locked and barred ; but as
about thirty half-starved, excited men came
in at the gate, the mother, who had made her
own plans, unfastened the door, ordering us
to lock it behind her, and stood outside alone
to meet and greet them. They stopped in
surprise. Then, 'Come on, lads ; we're noan
boun' to be done !' Looking up at them she
said, 'What's it all about ? What do you
want ?' 'We're clemming, missus !' 'Poor
chaps ! you look like it.' At that moment a

side window opened, and there stood on a sill
rows of pint pots filled with good steaming
stew—not soup, but stew, thick with the gristle
and meat of many shin-bones. 'Here! take
your fill'; 'and Tom,' pointing to our own
workman skulking behind the others, 'please
lift that clothes-basket through the window and
put it down.' It was filled with thick hunches
of bread. Again and again were the pots re-
filled. Did they soften and express gratitude?
No; not outwardly, anyway; but they took all
with rather a sullen air, as if baulked of some
set purpose of taking by force rather than
receiving of charity. The first plan would not
have hurt their pride so much, for there is a
heap of the 'stalk of carle hemp' in a
Lancashire lad."

With this epic scene we couple another from
the same source; together they make a vivid
and pathetic picture of poor life in Lancashire
under Protection: "One morning a decent
woman, whom we knew well, came, with her
white-faced little boy, for some 'broth.' A
quart of that, most likely all that she and her

four children would taste till next day. As
to the fathers, one of the most pathetic and
heart-breaking sights was to see in their drawn
features evidence how they pinched themselves
to let 'th' children an' th' missus have a sup.'
A grown man's craving hunger defied for love's
sake !

"Well, the can filled, she asked to speak to
the missus. 'What is it, Anne?'

"'Please, ma'm, would you let 'em save the
potatoe-peelings for me?'

"'Whatever for? You haven't got a pig?'

"'Eh no ; I wash 'em and chop 'em up, and
boil 'em with a handful of meal and a pinch of
salt, and th' childer like it well ; and please I'd
be thankful for any apple-peelings too. I boil
'em with a spoonful of treacle and a crust, if I
have it.' With tears in her eyes my mother
gave orders to 'save the peelings,' adding,
'Jane, peel them thick.' The week's accumu-
lation of coffee-grounds and tea-leaves were
worth a long walk to fetch."

A further quotation illustrates the subdued
anarchy of the time. "I recollect," the writer

says, "some one saying, 'B—— has gone off, had to fly for his life.' B—— was a small corn-merchant, living in the country between Rochdale and Bury. In a barn by his house he kept sacks of corn and sold it retail to the country people, who took it to the flour-mill to be ground, every week running up the price, as 'he'd soon be sold out.' It leaked out that if B——'s barn was empty he had his house, in the attic, under the roof, in the cellars, full of good corn, and, said one, 'Not such mixed rubbish as would hardly bake, but good, sound stuff.' One morning a lad rushed into the house, 'Master, run! go hide! they are coming to fetch you!' The scared man saw in the distance a black, moving mass, and heard a roar of angry voices. On came the mob. B—— had flown, but the corn was there. In a twinkling the doors were forced, and soon, dragged forth in triumph, sacks were piled high in the yard. Leaving them open, they poured out the contents, filling bags, aprons, hats, caps, pockets, even boots and shoes with the precious grain. Suddenly, in the midst of the noise and scramble, came the scouts' alarm, 'The sojers are coming!' Helter-skelter went the crowd, carrying off their spoil. When the soldiers arrived they found a wrecked house, a yard snowed over with corn, and a few sacks still unopened. Even then the grain had been so long kept and got damp, that it had to be mixed with a portion of sound flour to make it usable at all."

PROTECTION IN OTHER DISTRICTS

CHAPTER VI

PROTECTION IN OTHER DISTRICTS

SCOTLAND, Wales, and Ireland, together with certain counties of England, have sent us but few letters. These, together with one or two dealing with general conditions without specifying any particular locality, we have grouped together by themselves in this chapter. There is enough in them to confirm, if confirmation were needed, the conviction that Protection produced very much the same evils in every locality and under all circumstances. Several of them are exceedingly interesting, one letter from Aberdeen making us regret the general silence of Scotland.

A reader of the *Christian World*, who, unfortunately, gives no dates or places, says :

—" Families of growing sons and daughters never got a batch of good bread. Those were ' Protection times.' Talk of living ! It was more like a lingering death ! Sugar at that time was 6d. per lb., tea 1/- per quarter, 2 oz. having to serve a family a week ; should they be fortunate enough to run a cow on a common to get a little milk to improve the poor tea. No fiscal Joe's 3 acres and a cow in those good old days. The potatoe disease, too, set in about these times, making matters much worse for the working classes. Can it be wondered at that swedes were stolen from the fields to be eaten for food, or a pot of small potatoes, which had been boiled for pigs, disappearing in the same manner, or a dish of boiled peas being stealthily devoured by several poor hungry lads from their aunt's pantry, done while playing at hide and seek. There were sometimes religious fast days, which were almost a treat, as on those days we were not obliged to eat the only kind of bread to be got.

" A few days ago I noticed a farmer feeding his geese and poultry with damaged corn and other refuse from the threshing-floor, and I remarked to the man that the stuff he was giving the fowls was the same sort our bread was made from when I was a boy.

" At the time of the repeal of the Corn Laws, and soon after, we had to work from 4 a.m. until 6 and 8 p.m., lads for 4d. per day, and men, with wife and eight or nine children, for 9/- per week, and out of this meagre wage would be rent to pay and coal to buy. The wives had to wait up until a late hour on Saturday eve until father got home with the product of his week's labour, such as it was, consisting of a piece of fat bacon to boil. This was our only meat even for Sunday. The bread for the next week was frequently baked during the Sabbath day. If the batch did not hold out to the following Saturday or Sunday, then the pig's bag must be robbed (if there was one) of a little bran, sharps, or meal, or a little of each, which would serve in the shape of cakes when baked, and was in reality almost as good to eat as our bread, which, instead of 'rising' in the oven in the usual way, had a serious tendency to run all together and form one flat cake of about 3 or 4 inches in thickness, of a dark brown colour. Sometimes this would have to be cut out of the oven, or its top scooped out with the ladle.

"The above particulars, *i.e.*, long hours and small pay, reminds one of the following incident : 'As the master smith's apprentice was going to bed, his master reminded him not to forget to say his prayers. To make sure that the boy did this, the master listened on the stairs, and this was the prayer he heard the poor lad offer : "Our Father, which art in heaven. Oh!" he exclaimed, "if Thou art in heaven, stay there, for there is nothing here but hammer and smite from 4 in the morning till 8 at night."'"

Here is another letter, published in January, 1904, by the *Daily News*, in which, unfortunately, the writer gives no indication as to the particular part of the country referred to :—

" SIR,—I saw the other day in your valuable
and ever-welcome paper that Lord Rosebery
advocated the evidence, either orally or by
correspondence, of those who could remember
the bad old days of Protection.   Thinking
possibly that my experience may bring conviction to the class from which I sprung—the
working class—with whom the final question
of a return to Protection rests, although in my
77th year, I will ask you, Mr. Editor, to insert
this letter.

" I went apprentice, in 1841, in a Tory newspaper office, although the son of a staunch
Liberal and a subscriber to the 'Anti-Corn
Law League Journal.'   I therefore watched
the whole course of the struggle until the
final repeal of the odious Corn Laws.   What
I learnt at home and what I observed at the
office confirmed me in my faith, and I found
myself by and by combating the arguments of
my fellow-apprentices.   But there was a more
potent adversary at home to hasten their con-
version.   The price of bread went up to
1s. 2d. per loaf, and almost every article of

food followed suit; and of my own knowledge I knew that some of our apprentices tasted meat but once a week. The ready reader of this will say, 'Ah, that was on Sundays.' No, it was not. The family had to make their Sunday's dinner of hot vegetables; the meat was consumed on Mondays—cold.

"In our office the men's wages were 12s. and 14s. per week; the boys began with 1s. 6d. and finished with 6s. the seventh year. In 1845, I think, news was brought to the office that a farmer in our market had refused 16s. a bushel for his wheat, adding, as he buttoned up his sample in his capacious pocket, 'Not likely; it will be a guinea next week.' That night a raid was made upon his farm by the people, and but for the timely arrival of a company of the 3rd Light Dragoons his well-filled garner would have become smouldering ashes. In 1846 riots began, and the bakers' shops suffered; persons (some of the better class) being sent to prison for espousing the cause of the poor.

"Much more could I write, but the above may be taken as a fair sample of what took place, not only in our city, but in the country as well. Then came the Repeal of the Corn Laws, and I became a journeyman. I vividly retain the recollection of an incident not without significance even to the Protectionist of to-day. After repeal prices of food went down, trade became brisk, money more plentiful, and joy prevailed where before all was gloom and care. Wages were rising, and on March 6, 1848, I visited my employer to announce the fact that I was a journeyman. 'Well,' he said, 'you'll go on with the present rate of wages, of course?' I demurred, and hinted that wages all over the country were rising—Bristol was paying 26s. 'Ah,' he said, controversially, 'but, setting aside the part our paper took during the struggle, you can live now cheaper by 50 per cent. than you could then.' *Verbum sap.*—Yours, &c., C. S."

Mr. J. S. Baxter, of Burton Steps, Duke's Road, W.C., writes a letter illustrative of the condition of things in Lincolnshire :—

" Born of Tory parents, in 1826, at the
Spread Eagle Hotel, near the 'Stone Boar'
at Lincoln, I must now be 78. My parents
left there about 1830, and resided at Newark-
on-Trent, where my school days were spent.
At the age of fourteen I was apprenticed to
a manufacturing ironmonger at Sleaford, in
Lincolnshire, until the age of 21. It is during
that interval I well remember tea 8/- per lb.,
and sugar at preserving time 1/6 per lb., bread
8d., 1/-, and 1/6 per quartern loaf; and
although children of well-to-do parents, we
were stinted as to our rations of bread, and
not allowed sugar in our tea. The poor people
used to come to us clamouring for the tea-
leaves which had already done their duty well,
and the spare, dry crusts of bread. Chartists
and rioters came from Nottingham into
Newark, parading the streets with penny
loaves dipped in blood carried on pikes, crying
'Bread or blood!' The four-horse coaches
were being stopped and robbed continually,
people being afraid to travel (my father was
a proprietor in two coaches). When nearing

my 21st birthday wheat was 120/- per quarter.
A relative of mine held his back, thinking it
would reach 160/· ; and wheat-stacks were
fired throughout Lincolnshire, people saying
if they could not obtain bread the rich should
not. Our prisons were being rapidly filled.
Were these good times for the farmer? No.
The landlords raised the rents because they
were doing so well.

" I was then a good-looking, handsome, but
conceited Conservative dandy, something like
the present date, being educated in a hotbed
of Toryism. I knew Mr. Gladstone in his
early days, and have seen red herrings thrown
in his and Duke of Newcastle's face when at
the hustings — red was the Tory colour.
Were it not for your space being valuable, I
could relate some startling episodes. I will
close with one. A tailor at Sleaford was
cowardly killed by a superintendent of police.
At the inquest a verdict of ' Justifiable homi-
cide ' was returned. The case was taken up
by Ernest Jones, whom I also well remember.
It was this affair that turned my Toryism of

infancy into my Radicalism of manhood and old age."

Comparatively little light has also been thrown on matters from Scotland, Ireland, and Wales. Mr. John Bruce, of 358, Great Western Road, Aberdeen, writes : " I was born in 1816, and lived 4 years under George III., and remember when he died in 1820. I remember the Catholic Emancipation Bill in 1829, passed by the late Duke of Wellington and Sir Robert Peel ; also the excitement and great demonstrations that took place over the kingdom when the Reform Bill was passed in 1832. I was a journeyman baker (a youth of 17) when the late Mr. Gladstone made his first speech in the House of Commons, its purport being in favour of slavery.

" These were the days of cruel tyranny and small pay to the toiling mass. Every night the bakers had to begin work at 10 o'clock at night, and when the dough was made had a mouthful of supper and then lay down on the *bare boards*, with a sack above us, for an hour until the dough was ready, when we commenced and worked making bread and serving customers until seven or eight o'clock in the evening. No matter how short a time one had been in bed, they had to rise and begin work at 10 o'clock. Four of the journeymen, being married, were allowed to leave at 6 o'clock, and went home, returning at 10 o'clock. The bedroom that I and another young man had to sleep in being above the two ovens, the heat was simply suffocating in warm weather. The bed was full of bugs, that bit us so that on getting up our bodies were one mass of blisters, and so sick that we vomited for a considerable time, as the whole of the bakehouses in those days were underground. Some twenty years ago a doctor who was sanitary inspector of a certain district, raised an objection against these low bake-houses, and this having come under my notice, I at once wrote the Dr., and sent him a deal of information of the sort needed, and whose letters I yet retain expressing his gratitude, the result being that the whole of these underground bakehouses were dismantled.

"Worn out with cruel toil and poor pay, I left London early in 1836 and returned to Aberdeen till 1838, as the single men received bed and board from their employer. My wages *as foreman* was 7/- per week, bread and milk for breakfast, skate or herring and potatoes for dinner, and 'pulp' and bread for supper, and had to rise at 4 o'clock every morning and at 3 o'clock on Saturday. After I had been in business for some time, I proposed paying my men a money wage, allowing them to board where they chose. Other men, hearing of this, made a similar claim, and which the masters resented. It was won, however, and that work shouldn't begin till 5 o'clock instead of 4 o'clock. The four-pound loaf in those days ranged in price from 8d. to 11d., and, if I remember rightly, cost the latter sum when 'Free Trade' was won. I was a member of the Cobden Club, and attended every meeting when he visited Aberdeen, from its commencement to its termination, Joseph Chamberlain then being an advanced Radical and ardent Free Trader. Being a warm admirer of his, I retained a number of his speeches, particularly the one he delivered in Birmingham in 1884, while supporting the late John Bright at a Free Trade meeting. Having watched Chamberlain's conduct at the beginning of the war, I will ever maintain that but for him there would have been no war; and now that the war is over he has once more thrown the nation into a state of tumult owing to his proposal to lay aside *Free Trade*, and to adopt *Protection* once more, that proved such a bane and a curse, while Free Trade has been found such a blessing to the nation. In Protection days the wages of farm servants,[1] foremen horsemen received £4 for 6 months, second ditto £3 10s., and third ditto £3, while females received 25/- to 30/- for the same time. Tea was 6/- to 7/6 per pound, while the cheapest sugar cost 8d. per pound, while loaf 1/3, and whisky (not the sort maddening men to kill their wives as is common to-day) 2½d. per gill and to-day 8d. Aberdeen had two

---

[1] Presumably Mr. Bruce means in the neighbourhood of Aberdeen.

newspapers, the *Journal* (and which still exists) and the *Herald*, now substituted by the *Free Press*, the one published on Wednesday and the other on Saturday, and cost 7d. each. A letter to Inverurie cost 5½d., and to London 1/3½. To show the power exercised by the aristocracy in these dark days, they not only had their letters and correspondence passed through the Post Office free, but were granted the liberty of *franking* (as it was called) a letter or paper for any one, and which also passed through the Post Office free. To such an extent was this privilege abused that their women-folks were sending their lap dogs and fancy birds through the post free, when after a while a new postmaster put an end to it. Owing to work being scarce, low wages, and dear food, riots were continually taking place in all the big towns in the South, when the soldiers had to be called out. On one occasion the cavalry had to use their sabres ere peace could be restored. Chartism was rampant, and a report having been spread that a large number of them were coming to Aberdeen from the South, a large number of citizens were sworn in (of which I was one) as special constables, and for three nights on end we had to tramp the streets. Nothing came of it, however.

"In these hateful times the several guilds had the power to prevent any *extranear* (i.e., a stranger, or one not a Freeman, or that had not served a seven years' apprenticeship with a Freeman) to open a shop. I being one of these, was made to pay a fine on three occasions. I and a few others in a similar position determined that we should be free of this cruel tyranny, wrote the late Joseph Hume, M.P. for Montrose, explaining our position and asking his advice. He bade us correspond with all the other Royal boroughs of Scotland, get as many petitions numerously signed as possible, and send them to him not later than the 30th August, when the big folks would be leaving for their shootings. This we did, and shortly after the whole boroughs were thrown open.

"Now in my 88 year, sight and memory

failing, and having written my long letter at different times, it is not only sadly disconnected, but full of many errors, which kindly forgive. Land and liquor are the two things that have long damned society, and never can society be improved until they are sternly grappled with."

Irishmen must have suffered more than others under Protection. Indeed, it was the failure of the Irish potato crop that compelled Sir Robert Peel to remove the Corn Tax. The writer of the following letter might perhaps have given us more details of Irish life in the forties, but there are perhaps horrors enough in these letters without having details of the Irish famine. Admirers of Mr. Chamberlain should, however, remember that behind the England of our letters, with its poverty and hunger, there was a yet more miserable country than England. What Ireland was like in the forties can hardly be imagined.

" I am afraid there are few survivors of that period of over a half a century ago, who had ocular demonstration of the terrible scenes witnessed in these islands, when the ports were blockaded by heavy tariffs, against the importation of cheap food for the people.

"I, however, have lived through it; and date my acquaintance from 1849, with the grim signs and dark forebodings that threatened a national and violent revolution.

"The great Chartist movement was nothing more than a fierce revolt against low wages and dear food. The sweating and grinding of labour were a disgrace even to the lowest form of civilisation.

"Those who are living to-day have not the remotest idea of the miserable conditions of life, and of the bitter suffering, to which the mass of the people were subjected, through the pangs of poverty and the wild struggle for existence.

"How the toiling classes subsisted at all, under the shadow of a huge monopoly that crushed *Free Trade* and deprived them of the right of the natural expansion of their energies and their talents, is a problem that requires solving. The only thing that absolutely saved them occasionally from famine was the low rentals, that could not be otherwise under the hard and strange circumstances. In the cold winter, when the prevalence of frost and snow added to the terrors of the situation, I have seen them in groups and gangs, parading the streets of London, with hunger written on their faces, objects of pity, appealing for charity. Bad as they were, in the provincial towns they suffered more. The clamorous and silent victims of a criminal fiscal policy were everywhere. Riots were of daily occurrence, the military called out, and desperate encounters took place, always ending in bloodshed.

"Such was the state of Merry England in the happy days of Protection.

" But heartrending as the sights were in London and the towns, away in the rural districts the miseries endured by the peasantry were more pathetic and impressive. Subjugated by the landlords, whose tyrranny was awfull, they bore, with depressing patience, the hard lot to which they were assigned. But the flow of that patience was often interupted, when hayricks were flaming and the game preserves of the gentry ravaged.   With wheat at £2 15s. per quarter, and clover at £7 per ton, yet, although the prices of all farm produce ranged high in proportion, the unfortunate serf, bound to the soil, was, on the average, receiving only seven shillings per week.   The families were living in a state for which you find a comparison in the development of primitive man.   Their diet was the meanest, and scanty, and barely sufficient to hold together body and soul, consisting of vegetables, bad brown bread, and inferior fat bacon, in small quantities; and their dwellings were rotten structures in which whole generations lived and died in squalid misery.

" But of all the pictures of human woes and sorrows, Ireland, where I was born, in those eventful and unforgotten days, presented the darkest and most repulsive features.   All the dreadful afflictions, in the shapes of famine, starvation, and plague, which made humanity shudder, could be directly traced to the insane and dangerous laws that fettered and paralysed the industries of the people, by maintaining wicked and cruel tariffs that robbed the brightest of mankind of the right to live.

"But here I stop, as this letter is already too long.—Yours truly, "M. GRENY,

"25, Pearson Street, Kingsland Road, N.E.

"I subjoin a few items respecting the prices of food and labour, taken from memory, and for the correctness of which I pledge myself, and which may be of some interest to you.

					s.	d.
Tea, per lb.	...	...	...	...	4	0
Coffee, per lb.	...	...	...	...	3	0
Sugar, brown, per lb.	...	...	...	0	6
Sugar, loaf, per lb	...	...	...	0	7
Bread, 4-lb. loaf...	...	...	...	0	10

"All other articles of consumtion proportionately high.

Skilled workman	...	...	28s. weekly.
Unskilled workman	...	...	15s. ,,
Policeman	...	...	...	18s. ,,
Tailors, good hands, from 10s. to 20s. ,,

(From 12 to 16 hours a day.)

" This rate ruled in London, but much lower in the provinces."

This, from Mr. Samuel Nuttall, of Holywell, is our only letter from Wales :—

" The writer is now in his 71st year, and well remembers what he states of that time, from 1846. He well remembers the price of sugar, sandy in colour, at 9d. per lb., loaf sugar 1/2 per lb., and the price of other commodities of food at very high and prohibitive prices for the poor. I was the son of a small farmer, and fared better than many a one, as we had plenty of food, as it was ; but we were very hard up many a time, although we fared well. Our rent was repeatedly risen, should there happen to be a fair crop on the land. Many a time I remember poor people—and nearly everybody was poor—coming to my home to beg a few turnips to make broth. And what a broth ! I give you a simple receipt. Perhaps I had better describe the bread. At the time it was barley bread, and that very sour as a rule. When the harvest happened to be bad, that bread could not be kneaded properly, and when baked the outer crust was very hard. The inside was like clay, and smelt. In trying to cut it, it was sticking to the knife like glue. This was the kind of bread used for food. Now for the broth. The turnips were boiled, and when ready, the liquid, *i.e.*, the water, was poured on the bread, then flavoured with salt and pepper—when it could be had ; not a morsel of meat or anything else in. Here is another kind of broth. A herring was placed on the potatoes when boiling, and the liquid of this also was a dainty that those gentlemen who now wish to put on taxes on the food of the poor should be fed with for a month or two. I remember myself having some of the bread I have described in broth or milk. It stuck to the roof of my mouth, and the only way to get it off was by taking the handle end of the spoon to loosen it from the roof. The only white or wheaten bread we had was a small loaf, the price of which was 2d., for tea on Sunday, and that was cut very thin and placed between two slices of black bread, and we thought we had luxuries. The

families that could afford 2 or 3 lbs. of fresh
meat on Sunday were looked on as very
high livers indeed.   Children and women
(mothers) were begging a little lard or dripping
to put on the bread instead of butter, and a
pound of sugar had to last for a week, and
sometimes for a fortnight.   Tea was bought by
the ¼ of an ounce, the price being about 6/-
a pound.   Bread and black treacle was the food
of children, and, in many cases, of whole
families.

   " Clothing was very scarce. The same clothes
had to do for all the boys that happened to be
of the same family and near the same size,
wearing them alternately when going from
home, or to church or chapel. Some were
fairly fit, and others were much too large for
the wearers, and some the other way ; some
with trousers turned up, others too short by
about 10 inches. The sleeves of the coats
were similar, and to see grown-up people in
these garments would astonish the food taxers,
I presume.

   " The wages of the best farm servants

(males) was 5/- per week and food, the lower
ones was 6d. and 7d.   The men kept on large
farms to thresh the corn earned from 5/- to 7/-
per week.   There were no threshing machines
then, only human ones, and it was their work
all round the year. The wages of lead miners—
and there were a good many in these parts—was
7/- to 9/- a week, and if a miner could get 10/-
per week he was considered   very lucky
indeed.

" The plight of mostly all the working classes
was pitiful.   The only mode of illumination at
that time was by candles ! And what candles !
They were what was called "dips," and they
were used very sparing—most of the nights
were passed in the dark.   The only light they
had was that of a small fire, doing most of their
work in the dark, some burning half a candle,
others an inch or two.   The parties that could
have a candle to burn until bedtime were
lucky.

" I remember many other sad things of those
hard times ; but perhaps it is as advisable that
I should draw an end here."

THE ENGLAND OF THE LETTERS

CHAPTER VII

THE ENGLAND OF THE LETTERS

(By Brougham Villiers)

THE letters printed in the foregoing chapters read like the records of a besieged city. They describe a state of things enduring not for a few weeks, but for a full generation, in which the tragedy of poverty had become nearly universal, in which the "submerged tenth" of our own day was nearly co-extensive with the nation. Upon the whole, we are convinced, our country has never passed through so terrible a time before or since. Right through the Middle Ages sporadic famines occurred, and there were years of terrible dearth, due to defective harvests; but so continuous a period of systematic underfeeding of the whole nation never before occurred. Sooth to say, there was some foundation for the plentiful beef and ale with which we, as a people, were once credited. Thorold Rogers and Professor Ashley alike insist that the England of the Middle Ages was well fed. The peasantry of early Plantagenet times, according to the latter, lived in a state of " rude plenty," while Rogers has extolled the fifteenth century as the " golden age " of the British working man.

But from the time of the Reformation there had been a steady decline in the material well-being of the British working class. Their organisations had been broken up in the villages, and had become, in the towns, close corporations, to which the poor man had no access. He was left to face the difficulties of the Industrial Revolution with no trade or other organisations of his own, and with the machinery of the State in the hands of the class most hostile to him. The great war with France had raised corn to famine prices, and accustomed the landlords to enormous rent-rolls, which they desired to retain in time of peace. This could only be done by some system reproducing the economic conditions which the termination of the war would otherwise have ended. In other words, the island, since it was not now besieged by its enemies, must be besieged by its rulers. Tariffs must undo the mischief wrought by the peace and make dear the produce of the land.

The calamity which the Corn Laws inflicted on the people found them rather prepared to endure than to resist. On the one hand they had, as we have seen, no organisation nor political power. The protests of the working classes, as such, then, could only take a form essentially anarchic in character. There is no doubt that, from the first, they were bitterly opposed to the bread tax ; but their only means of resisting it were by bread riots and chronic law-breaking. But unfortunately, as we have said, if they had little power to resist, the working classes were better fitted than at any other time to endure. Probably at no time in our history was the poor man of so little account as during the seventeenth and eighteenth centuries. With, as we have said, no organisations of his own, no institution in village or nation in the control of which his voice counted for anything, he was used to doing everything on the orders of his "betters," and had come to acquiesce in a view of life which virtually regarded him as outside the pale of civilisation. For him the "polite letters" of the eighteenth century did not exist. The philosophers regarded him as quite beneath the range of their ideas. Religions were all "to philosophers equally false, to the vulgar equally true, to Statesmen equally useful," *i.e.*, to keep the people in their place. These words of Gibbon express the general attitude of the most advanced thought to the common people. The people themselves had for several generations been driven to solve the problem of living under, on the whole, harder and harder conditions. Their hours had become longer, and their wages, relatively to the price of food, lower and lower with each generation. A thoroughly vicious poor law had completed the work begun by the destruction of their democratic organisations, and accustomed them to look for work and charity, not to themselves and their fellows, but to the contemptuous patronage of the squires. They had learnt much already of the expedients of penury ; they had lost almost the instinct and entirely the practice of mutual aid. They were, therefore, equally fitted to bear and unfitted to resist a new oppression and still sterner poverty.

Of all this the letters bear abundant traces, however the changed conditions of their later lives may have altered the outlook of the writers. We get a vivid picture of the reality of the struggle with poverty. We see the pitiful expedients resorted to to obtain a substitute for tea. Burnt crusts, dried herbs, or old tea-leaves, were begged from the houses of well-to-do people. We hear of families buying $\frac{1}{2}$ oz. of tea for a week, and these not among slum-dwellers, but among regularly employed, respectable work people. Tea, one of the commonest luxuries of the poor now, indeed the only luxury of many thousands, plays what

17

will appear to some readers an unduly prominent part in the correspondence. It is, as we have said, almost the only luxury of many poor people, and the time when tea could not be obtained seems to them almost as horrible to look back upon as the days of dear bread. As bread is the peasant woman's prime necessity, so tea is her chief comfort; without the one life could not be, without the other it would be much more dreary than those who have many other luxuries imagine. Thus it is that there is a real pathos about these pitiful attempts we read of to provide a substitute, and that we so often find this comfort specified among those things of which but a little could be bought.

The letters raise our curiosity as to what, under Protection, was really the staple food of the people. Cobbett feared that England would submit to be fed on the detested potato. In his time there was clearly a tendency to substitute for dear bread this cheaper food. Indeed, Cobbett hardly thinks of the potato as a *vegetable*, as it is used now, but as a possible substitute for bread and bacon, the proper food, in his opinion, of the cottager. A quotation from a nearly contemporary pamphlet which has come into our hands states that "potatoes are almost the sole food of labouring poor, because the cheapest. No man can do a good day's work, or be kept in health and strength, under ten pounds during 24 hours." The writer then estimates the expenses of a labourer's family, where the man is constantly employed at 8s. a week, and has a wife and two children, as follows :—

	£	s.	d.
Potatoes	8	0	0
Cottage or Lodgings	3	3	0
Shoes and repairs for labourer, 12s.; for wife and family, 8s.	1	0	0
Various articles and clothing—labourer, £2 5s.; family, £1 10s.	3	15	0
Fuel	1	0	0
	£16	18	0

" This leaves," he says, " a surplus of £3 18s. to furnish tools, candles, soap, and numerous little articles. It is to be recollected that the above statement confines the diet of the labourer and family exclusively to potatoes and water, instead of allowing him the more expensive luxury of bread, and supposes him to be regularly employed during the whole year, when the fact is that this is not the happy lot of more than half the class!" This family budget appears rather fanciful, as it seems rather much, even for a rural labourer, to eat ten pounds of potatoes in a day; but it is clear that the tendency which Cobbett feared, to substitute potatoes for bread, had made some progress in the ten years between the publication of "Cottage Economy" and this pamphlet.

That the cheap potato played a much larger part in the feeding of the people than at present, is clear from many of the letters. There are many cases where the dinner of the family was confined to potatoes, with a little lard or dripping; and it appears that when the coming of the potato disease and the repeal of the Corn Laws arrested the process, the English working classes were rapidly being driven to make their staple food of the potato. The

invective of Cobbett probably voiced a good
deal of real popular feeling, but the point to
note is that though he foresaw the danger, yet,
as late as 1824, the substitution seems not to
have proceeded anything like so far as it had
even ten or twenty years later, otherwise he
would have pointed out more clearly the extent
of the abuse.   He seems to have considered
that the people mainly lived upon bread in
spite of the encroachments of the hated root.

Even when the people did get bread it was
not always made from wheat. We see little
barley bread nowadays, and, to judge from our
letters, this is not to be wondered at.   It seems
to have obtained a peculiarly evil reputation,
not shared by apparently coarser substitutes for
wheat, like oats and rye.   "You do not know
what heartburn means till you have eaten
barley bread," says one correspondent, and it
is evident, from the manner in which it is
usually spoken of, that the barley bread was
hard to digest.   Cobbett, on the other hand,
advised it ; and as he is a sincere well-wisher
of the cottager according to his lights—that is

to say he wished him to have plenty of solid food and country sports, with no fancy book-learning, theatres, or town fashions—we must suppose that it was not always so bad. Probably the truth is that barley bread, unless the grain has been well won, is worse than others, and that in the fiery hatred against it, of which the reader will find proof in the letters themselves, we have an echo of the bad harvests of the late thirties, at the beginning of Cobden's campaign. One thing is clear, it is a very bad thing to be driven back on English-grown barley for a staple food in view of the uncertainty of the national climate. These people who found barley bread so hard to digest are men and women, for the most part, of better than the average constitution, or else they would not have lived to contribute to the "Hungry Forties." If *they* remember the terrors of barley bread all these years, what must their more delicate brothers and sisters have suffered ?

But there was a danger that the English people would be driven to yet lower kinds of food than potatoes or barley bread. The prominent part that swede turnips played in the diet of the people will probably strike most readers with horror. Here, indeed, we come to a food basis on which it seems impossible that healthy life can be maintained. Even now turnips are not infrequently resorted to by the unfortunate dwellers in our city slums, who in this respect are even worse off than their forefathers. The turnip is the last refuge of desperate poverty, for as long as there is any money with which to buy food, it is almost certain to be spent on something better. But it is much easier, especially in the country, to steal a turnip for dinner than almost anything else. Only one big one need be taken at a time, and after it has been taken up, and the poor thief is off the field, it is impossible for any one to prove that it has not just been picked up off the road. Instances have come to our own knowledge where families in city slums have lived for several days on turnips stolen nightly from the nearest fields. This manner of living appears to have been much more common during the forties, however, and there are many instances in the letters of families having turnips only for dinner. That they were sometimes, probably often, stolen is clear, but it does not, of course, follow that they were always so. There must have been a good deal of give-and-take charity in those days, and probably the hardest farmers would not refuse to give away a swede or two to any one who begged for them.

How hard a struggle the people had to clothe themselves can well be imagined. It was here, indeed, that the Corn Laws hit the cotton and woollen manufacturers so hardly. After the people had bought enough of the coarsest food they hardly could have any money left for anything else. How they got clothed at all is a mystery. We read of lads sitting in bed on Sunday to patch a pair of trousers for the week; of farmers going to church in clothes which the modern labourer would hardly appear in on a week-day, and of places where hardly any of the men had a waistcoat unless they had collected enough mole-skins to make one. It is here, in fact, that we first realise that our comparison of " Protected " England to a besieged city is not entirely adequate. A siege of moderate duration, however it may distress the people for food, does not necessarily raise in an acute form the problem of clothing. Old garments may be made to do till the siege ends, one way or other. But from the beginning of the French War until the repeal of the Corn Laws, a period of sixty years, this country was in a state of semi-siege. During the whole of that time an underfed people had to buy every article of clothing at the cost of further severe privation in feeding. Everything was bought at the expense of a hard sacrifice elsewhere. It is no wonder, then, that the manufacturers of Manchester and Leeds found the home market inelastic, and that when, through improved machinery, they had cheapened the price of textiles, they were not recouped by increased sales.

Working-class women, heavily burdened as they are now, were terribly oppressed in

Protection times. It must not be supposed that there is any one case in the letters of feminine overwork that could not too probably be paralleled in some cases now, but certainly things were much worse then. Our letters give instances of women going out to severe work in the fields at sixpence a day, within a few days of childbirth; of a woman being brutally beaten by an estate bailiff, of another crying at the price of bread. The tragedy of a poor man's wife must have been very bitter in the forties. Even on the wages of a modern mechanic in full employ, the task of making both ends meet every week is one of which too few people realise the dreary difficulty. How it is done we confess we do not know; and the fact that so many working women manage to rear families on even moderately good wages, like thirty or forty shillings a week, without getting into debt, is one that has always filled us with the deepest admiration and respect. Capacity for affairs can be as clearly shown on a small scale as on a great, and we consider this relatively common achievement a striking proof of a capacity for management too rarely admitted.

But if the balancing of the present working-class budget be a feat of management, what must it have been in the forties? Briefly, we think, one of the most terrible and heartbreaking tasks ever imposed on human-kind. What, we suspect, lightens the burden of ways and means to women, is the possibility of squeezing sixpence or a shilling out for some little extra, some treat in the food line, or a little to save towards buying a coveted ornamental or useful article for the house. But every such solace was denied to the poor woman who, with bread at 1s. a quartern loaf, had to feed a family on a wage of six or eight shillings a week. Before her lay only the hope of avoiding starvation; underfeeding to some extent was inevitable, having even a penny to spare to gratify any fancy of her own was out of the question. She had to manage her house, make a balance somehow, and work outside for dear life as well. It is no wonder, then, that the women play a prominent part in our letters. Their mental and bodily suffering must have been truly awful.   One shudders to think of it.

There are many pictures of startling pathos in the letters.   Perhaps the most poignant is that of the Dorsetshire labourer and his wife "crying like babies" as their child eat their one crust, softened in hot water, with the eagerness of a long day's fast.   We have the case of the woman crying because she could get no more than a bloater for her overworked husband's dinner.   But, indeed, these pages are wet with the tears of women and children, as they are lightened with many instances of devoted unselfishness on the part of parents.   The letters bear witness to the deep, subdued anarchy of the time, of the rioting, rick-burning, poaching, and general lawlessness of the starving people.   Sometimes there are epic glimpses of primitive violence.   The picture of the house-mother standing outside her door, and feeding with stew and bread a body of riotous Lancashire men, stands out as from the pages of some Iceland saga, and seems strangely out of place to those accustomed to the bourgeois order of the later nineteenth century. But unless we fix our eyes on the anarchic character of the period, we have not grasped the full horror of the Corn Tax. In spite of the long years intervening since their childhood, the writers echo the tone of the time when they were young. They bring to politics a spirit well-nigh dead, the spirit of moral indignation against oppression. The oppressions that exist now have a less obvious source; they are either less widely diffused or caused by a less crude form of selfishness. The people suffer from them, but they do not trace so clearly their cause to an obvious source; their privations seem rather due to the cruelty of nature than of law, and hence they do not arouse such a spirit of lawlessness.

"He that withholdeth the corn, the people shall curse him; but blessing shall be upon the head of him that selleth it." This proverb is the earliest instance, as we hope some of our letters are the last, of the long protest of the poor in history against those who make dear the bread of the people. In the Middle Ages we meet with the same feeling in the public horror of "regrators" and "forestallers," and we find the permanent sentiment preserved in the legend of the wicked Bishop Hatto, eaten by rats as a judgment for the same sin. For, indeed, the poor will make many allowances for their rulers. Laws may oppress, but, though they may feel them hard, they have often been only too ready to think they may be just, however stern. They are prepared, at any rate, to make allowances for their rulers' point of view, to think that, even if they are wrong, they may at least be honest. But though it is probable enough that the statesmen who imposed the Corn Tax were quite as honest as those who support any other injustice, and that regrators were probably no more heartless than other speculators, their offence was one which the people have always seen clearly. When by any means his bread is made dearer to him, the labourer does not think the causer of dearth mistaken, he considers him wicked. Men may submit to the most arbitrary punishment and think it just, the slave may be obsessed so as to believe he really does belong to another, but the poor have always stood out against the injustice of dear bread. The old-world instances just quoted are paralleled by many stories in these letters. We read of a farmer who held his corn for a rise till it was eaten by rats, and we can imagine how the peasants talked of the "judgment" that had fallen upon him. One is reminded in reading of the story of Bishop Hatto, and wonders if some such fact had given rise to the legend.

But though the injustice of the bread tax was seen clearly enough by the people, and the poverty of the working-class was felt by the more sympathetic among the rich, there was an amazing anarchy of thought among those who felt most deeply the condition of England problem. We must remember that Carlyle was the leading social philosopher of the day, and it is instructive to find in his writing, along with the same moral indignation, the same constructive incapacity we observe almost everywhere else. Carlyle's essays of the time read like the voice of the nation, clearly seeing that everything was wrong, bitterly complaining of the inadequacy of all methods of reform suggested but hopeless in suggestion, except, according to Lowell's sarcastic phrase, that men "should sit down beside the cartman in the slough, and shout lustily for Hercules." Working men had then no wide-spread organisations of their own, for Chartism was too loose a thing to perform the function of the Trade Unions of to-day. Nor was Chartism always right. It largely failed to recognise in the Anti-Corn Law League the one really effective organisation dealing with one thing only, the first and most vital thing of all.

Now years of ripened experience, of successful work, we presume, in many cases, with their fellow-men have not quite eradicated the traces of the age of revolt from our writers. They feel the food question as a moral one with a thoroughness with which, it is to be feared, the present age feels nothing. But they are not nearly so eager to advance new constructive ideas as their younger friends would be. They belong to and echo the ideas of an age which was grappling with a deeply felt oppression, and could see nothing beyond the destruction of it. They preserve, in fact, the spirit of Carlyle, and do something to explain why he was looked upon, not only as a prophet, but as a sage.

That so many letters from all manner of writers should have been collected, shows clearly what a powerful force is fighting against the " Tariff Reformers " under the surface of things. The battle against the followers of Mr. Chamberlain is not conducted only on the platform and in the daily press. The letters here published, numerous as they are, have been written by a very small portion of the million or more of English men and women who remember the days of dear bread. To them, as we gather from the words of the fraction who here speak, the ordinary feeling we associate with all age is reversed. *They* do not look back on their youth as a day of delight which they recall with vain regret, but as an Egyptian bondage from which they have been delivered. And just such people are in every village in the land. We cannot doubt that during this last year of "hustle," a more quiet, but more effective propaganda was being carried on by many a chimney corner by those whose tongues were let loose on the sorrows of their youth. Just such tales as are here reproduced, little regarded as they might be at ordinary times, must have been made suddenly interesting by Mr. Chamberlain's plunge of last year, and must have been re-told again and again. Good work had been done by more famous people in defence of Free Trade, but much, perhaps, if we knew all, should be attributed to the unknown "gaffers" and "gammers" of the land who, if they never heard of "The Wealth of Nations," at least could speak of that they knew. We may, perhaps, gather from this book the true reason of the remarkable record of by-elections in 1904.

T. FISHER UNWIN, Publisher,

For Politicians and Students of Politics.

THE REFORMER'S BOOKSHELF.

Large crown 8vo, cloth, **3s. 6d.** *each.*

1. **The English Peasant: His Past and Present.** By RICHARD HEATH.

2. **The Labour Movement.** By L. T. HOBHOUSE, M.A. Preface by R. B. HALDANE, M.P.

3 & 4. **Sixty Years of an Agitator's Life:** GEO. JACOB HOLYOAKE's Autobiography. 2 vols.

5 & 6. **Bamford's Passages in the Life of a Radical.** Edited, and with an Introduction, by HENRY DUNCKLEY ("Verax"). 2 vols.

9 & 10. **The Economic Interpretation of History:** Lectures on Political Economy and its History, delivered at Oxford 1887–1888. By Prof. THOROLD ROGERS. Third Edition. 2 vols.

11 & 12. **The Industrial and Commercial History of England.** By Prof. THOROLD ROGERS. 2 vols.

13. **Nihilism as it is.** Being STEPNIAK's Pamphlet Translated by E. L. VOYNICH, and FELIX VOLKHOVSKY's " Claims of the Russian Liberals." With an Introduction by Dr. SPENCE WATSON.

14 & 15. **Charles Bradlaugh:** A Record of his Life and Work. By his Daughter, HYPATIA BRADLAUGH BONNER. 2 vols.

16 & 17. **The Inner Life of the House of Commons.** Selected from the Writings of WILLIAM WHITE, with a Prefatory Note by his Son, and an Introduction by JUSTIN McCARTHY, M.P.

18. **A Village Politician.** The Life Story of John Buckley. Edited by J. C. BUCKMASTER. With an Introduction by the Right Hon. A. J. MUNDELLA, M.P.

19 & 20. **Taxes on Knowledge:** The Story of their Origin and Repeal. By COLLET DOBSON COLLET. With an Introduction by GEORGE JACOB HOLYOAKE. 2 vols.

21 & 22. **Life of Richard Cobden.** By JOHN MORLEY. *2* vols.

23. **Cobden (Richard) and the Jubilee of Free Trade.** By P. LEROY-BEAULIEU, HENRY DUNCKLEY (" Verax "), Dr. THEODOR BARTH, the Right Hon. LEONARD COURTNEY, M.P., and the Right Hon. CHARLES VILLIERS, M.P. With Introduction by RICHARD GOWING, Secretary of the Cobden Club. Crown 8vo, cloth, uniform in style with the Jubilee Edition of " Richard Cobden."

BUILDERS OF GREATER BRITAIN

EDITED BY

H. F. WILSON

A Set of 10 *Volumes, each with Photogravure Frontispiece, and Map, large crown 8vo., cloth,* **5** *s. each.*

The completion of the Sixtieth year of the Queen's reign will be the occasion of much retrospect and review, in the course of which the great men who, under the auspices of Her Majesty and her predecessors, have helped to make the British Empire what it is to-day, will naturally be brought to mind. Hence the idea of the present series. These biographies, concise but full, popular but authoritative, have been designed with the view of giving in each case an adequate picture of the builder in relation to his work.

The series will be under the general editorship of Mr. H. F. Wilson formerly Fellow of Trinity College, Cambridge, and now private secretary to the Right Hon. J. Chamberlain at the Colonial Office. Each volume will be placed in competent hands, and will contain the best portrait obtainable of its subject, and a map showing his special contribution to the Imperial edifice. The first to appear will be a Life of Sir Walter Ralegh, by Major Hume, the learned author of "The Year after the Armada." Others in contemplation will deal with the Cabots, the quarter-centenary of whose sailing from Bristol is has recently been celebrated in that city, as well as in Canada and Newfoundland ; Sir Thomas Maitland, the "King Tom" of the Mediterranean ; Rajah Brooke, Sir Stamford Raffles, Lord Clive, Edward Gibbon Wakefield, Zachary Macaulay, &c., &c.

The Series has taken for its motto the Miltonic prayer :—

" 𝕿𝖍𝖔𝖚 𝖂𝖍𝖔 𝖔𝖋 𝕿𝖍𝖞 𝖋𝖗𝖊𝖊 𝖌𝖗𝖆𝖈𝖊 𝖉𝖎𝖉𝖘𝖙 𝖇𝖚𝖎𝖑𝖉 𝖚𝖕 𝖙𝖍𝖎𝖘 𝕭𝖗𝖎𝖙𝖙𝖆𝖓𝖓𝖎𝖈𝖐 𝕰𝖒𝖕𝖎𝖗𝖊 𝖙𝖔 𝖆 𝖌𝖑𝖔𝖗𝖎𝖔𝖚𝖘 𝖆𝖓𝖉 𝖊𝖓𝖛𝖎𝖆𝖇𝖑𝖊 𝖍𝖊𝖎𝖌𝖍𝖙𝖍, 𝖂𝖎𝖙𝖍 𝖆𝖑𝖑 𝖍𝖊𝖗 𝕯𝖆𝖚𝖌𝖍𝖙𝖊𝖗 𝕴𝖘𝖑𝖆𝖓𝖉𝖘 𝖆𝖇𝖔𝖚𝖙 𝖍𝖊𝖗, 𝖘𝖙𝖆𝖞 𝖚𝖘 𝖎𝖓 𝖙𝖍𝖎𝖘 𝖋𝖊𝖑𝖎𝖈𝖎𝖙𝖎𝖊."

1. **SIR WALTER RALEGH.** By MARTIN A. S. HUME, Author of "The Courtships of Queen Elizabeth," &c.

2. **SIR THOMAS MAITLAND;** the Mastery of the Mediterranean. By WALTER FREWEN LORD.

3. **JOHN CABOT AND HIS SONS; the Discovery of** North America. By C. RAYMOND BEAZLEY, M.A.

4. **EDWARD GIBBON WAKEFIELD; the Colonisation of South** Australia and New Zealand. By R. GARNETT, C.B., L.L.D.

5. **LORD CLIVE;** the Foundation of British Rule in India. By Sir A. J. ARBUTHNOT, K.C.S.I., C.I.E.

RAJAH BROOKE; the Englishman as Ruler of an Eastern State. By Sir SPENSER ST. JOHN, G.C.M.G.

ADMIRAL PHILIP; the Founding of New South Wales. By LOUIS BECKE and WALTER JEFFERY.

SIR STAMFORD RAFFLES; England in the Far East. By the Editor.

T. FISHER UNWIN, Publisher,

THE STORY OF
THE NATIONS

A SERIES OF POPULAR HISTORIES.

Each Volume is furnished with Maps, Illustrations, and Index. Large Crown 8vo, fancy cloth, gold lettered, or Library Edition, dark cloth, burnished red top, **5s.** *each.—Or may be had in half Persian, cloth sides, gilt tops ; Price on Application.*

11, Paternoster Buildings, London, E.C.

T. FISHER UNWIN, Publisher,

Recent Volumes in the

STORY OF THE NATIONS

A SERIES OF POPULAR HISTORIES.

Each Volume complete with Maps, many Illustrations, and an Index. Large crown 8vo, fancy cloth, gold lettered, or Library Edition, dark cloth, burnished red top, 5s. each. Or may be had in half Persian, cloth sides, gilt tops: Price on Application.

49. **Austria.** By SIDNEY WHITMAN.

50. **Modern England before the Reform Bill.** By JUSTIN MCCARTHY.

51. **China.** With a New Chapter on Recent Events. By Prof. R. K. DOUGLAS.

52. **Modern England under Queen Victoria.** By JUSTIN MCCARTHY.

53. **Modern Spain, 1878-1898.** By MARTIN A. S. HUME, F.R.H.S., Author of "Sir Walter Ralegh," &c.

54. **Modern Italy, 1748-1898.** By PIETRO ORSI, Professor of History in the R. Liceo Foscarini, Venice. With over 40 Illustrations and Maps.

55. **Norway.** By Professor HJALMAR H. BOYESEN, Author of "Idylls of Norway."

56. **Wales.** By OWEN EDWARDS.

IN PREPARATION.

The United States of America, 1783-1900. By A. C. M'LAUGHLIN. In 2 Volumes.

The Papal Monarchy: From Gregory the Great to Boniface VIII. By Rev. W. BARRY.

Mediæval Rome. By WILLIAM MILLER.

Buddhist India. By T. W. RHYS DAVIDS.

The Story of Greece (to the Roman Occupation). By E. S. SHUCKBURGH.

The Story of Greece (from the Roman Occupation to A.D. 1453). By E. S. SHUCKBURGH.

11, Paternoster Buildings, London, E.C.

The Gresham Press,
UNWIN BROTHERS, LIMITED,
WOKING AND LONDON.